O1

First contact & Personal disclosure

Walter Steading

By

Willard G. Van De Bogart

Table of Contents

Preface:

Preface:

I am writing this book to explain the psychological and physiological changes that come about as a result of experiencing a personal contact with either an unknown aerial phenomenon (UAP) or a form of intelligence that is not human and presumably not from planet earth. Having experienced many kinds of contacts myself I have decided to write about my changes and how I have come to cope and understand those changes and explain how I have dealt with them. I offer these personal insights because I know that many people have had contact experiences but do not know how to live with the experience nor can they have a dialogue about their contact experience with other people. As a result of having many contact experiences, I have decided to describe in detail some of the changes we potentially can experience and how to identify and understand those changes. Although many have told their story of abductions or face-to-face contact there is little discussion available on what exactly can happen to our state of mind or whether our body has changed from what it was before one had a contact experience.

This book hopes to fill that gap by addressing some profound considerations as a result of there being so many encounters with intelligence from other worlds or even other dimensions. A lengthy discussion will take place on the difference between a human and a non-human and whether there is the possibility that we have become hybrid humans even if we are a new kind of human. And lastly, would we be ready to accept the fact that we have become non-human persons? Is it possible to accept this other-worldly intelligence as part of who we are and whether we could tell if we were non-human and whether we could accept talking to or listening to another non-human person. These are existential questions that will have to be considered as our visitors or the others as I refer to them are appearing in greater number on our planet which begs the question of who they are and what they are doing here?

Willard G. Van De Bogart

Bangkok, Thailand

May 18, 2022

Email: vanflight@gmail.com

Introduction:

How humans make contact with extraterrestrials can happen in many different ways. This is a story about discovering others who are extraterrestrials living on earth. My history of receiving messages from other-worldly beings began in 1952 in Nahant, Massachusetts. I mentioned this first encounter in my first book, *Alien Child*. Since that time I have received many more messages in different forms such as direct sightings, telepathic encounters, and voices and sounds. Humans who have had a first contact experience with entities other than humans, is a widely known phenomenon. Many people around the world have had their experiences made into books and films. Travis Walton is one of the better-known cases of abduction with his book, *Fire in the Sky*, Whitley Strieber with his book, *Communion,* and Jacques Vallée with his book, *Trinity,* which is based on an eyewitness account of a crashed UFO in New Mexico. Many people who have had experiences with extraterrestrials have remained silent because of concerns of being socially ridiculed. In my book, *Alien Child,* I mentioned many of my own contact experiences, and how they affected me physically, emotionally, and psychologically. A major contact took place for me on Winter Solstice December 21, 2020, in Yucca Valley, California. The two weeks that followed that contact experience made me feel disoriented as if I had been transported to a new realm of existence and experienced many new forms of expressions, new ideas and a new fluidity in my thinking took place. With that experience. all my previous memories became extremely vivid and were mixed with experiences in the real world. The contact took place at 2:03 am on Dec. 21, 2020, under a starry sky in Yucca Valley, California at Garth's Boulder Garden while playing my electronic synthesizers. The contact experience resulted while using my voice with specific frequencies on my synthesizers. A symbiosis of my music and my entire body took place as if there was a unification between myself and entities living in the night sky. In this book, I will attempt to describe how we respond to the extraterrestrial phenomenon. Our minds act as filters to whatever is being communicated from these other beings. This contact experience at Yucca Valley, California and many more will be elaborated upon in this book.

Chapter One: Making Contact:

After my Yucca Valley contact experience, I discovered that making references to things in the world had changed dramatically. Attachment to concepts, philosophical positions, and cosmological pursuits had dissolved leaving me to invent who I was and where I was going in life. It became increasingly difficult for me to put any ideas into words, which I have enjoyed doing all my life. Only today, April 24, 2021, at 8:45 am do I feel compelled to try and explain the effects I have been experiencing since Dec. 21, 2020. It was at that time many celestial occurrences were taking place in the heavens. Those celestial events, as it turns out, had a profound effect on my whole life while living in this other-worldly reality. After several months had passed my mind felt like an empty chamber mixed with tones and ideas and even voices swimming in my mind. It was as if all the stars in heaven just appeared inside my head. Celestial sounds mixed with strange voices filled every part of me. I became a vessel of audible starlight. The more I experienced this state of star consciousness the more I identified with it until I could finally relate to the idea of star entities born out of the heavens. As I floated mentally in this new world new knowledge of existence became part of my whole being. The earth became a liquid fantasy with sound and colors fused creating a dynamic interplay of thoughts, and a new language born out of starlight and sounds that could be heard from all over the universe. I became elevated into a world composed of worlds all over the universe. It was as if I ascended into space where understanding had new inclusiveness, and all the time this was happening in my mind I was editing Sanskrit inscriptions in Bangkok in real time. The Sanskrit inscriptions related to a newer type of knowledge that was being translated by Chirapat Prapandvidya, the foremost Sanskrit scholar in SE Asia. In our collaboration, we reached a verse in the Sanskrit inscriptions that referred to how a certain type of knowledge was equated with some higher form of existence. The Sanskrit word used for higher could range from pinnacle, peak, top, or zenith. Hours went by trying to determine how best to translate what the poets in the 3rd century CE were trying to express. The Sanskrit was being translated into English, a first in inscription translations of which I was the associate editor for the book. Select Sanskrit Inscriptions in India and Southeast Asia Vol. 1, by Dr. Chirapat Prapandvidya.

At a particular junction in my translation work was when my perception of a new reality fused with the Sanskrit translation and opened up a state of mind the ancients seemed to be referring to. The abode of Shiva residing on Mt. Kailash, a high peak in the Kailash Range forming part of the trans-Himalaya area, came to mind. Mt. Kailash is the one place on earth that encourages all Hindus to make a pilgrimage to join in that rarefied place where Shiva resides.

4

At that instance, while doing the English translation, I heard voices calling out from the peaks of heaven asking me to join them to experience the knowledge of the heavens. Instantly the image of Mt. Shasta, California appeared in my mind's eye as I was editing the Sanskrit translations looking for the best word to describe the highest place of knowledge; the word zenith was finally chosen. The voices I heard coming from Mt. Shasta were the same voice that contacted me in those early morning hours in Yucca Valley, California on Dec. 21, 2020. What also came to mind were my Aboriginal Dreamtime experiences with deities from Proxima b when I visited Iga Warta, Australia with the aboriginal elder Clifford Coulthard. Clifford told me that it would take up to six months or more to fully understand the transmissions from their twin deities, the Valnaapa, which I later published in my book, Alien Child.

After these mental apparitions subsided I realized I had to go to a high peak to experience another transmission where once again I could exchange new ideas about being human in the universe while playing my electronic synthesizers. I was guided to go to Mt. Shasta, California, and as it turned out I eventually arrived at the Fowler campground in McCloud, California where I set up my tent in the forest at the base of Mt. Shasta on May 31, 2021. I had a premonition about Mt. Shasta months earlier when I was in Bangkok, Thailand, editing ancient Sanskrit and now I miraculously found myself in Mt. Shasta.

The Fowler campground was very quiet with the sun filtering down through the tree tops next to Mt. Shasta. So, I began writing every morning for two weeks in the early morning hours. At first, it seemed I was just exploring for answers. What kind of beings are we? Were we cosmically radiated by plasma fields that re-organized our very foundation of protein construction, or did a profound sound penetrate our being to attune us to cosmic stimulation to acquire some kind of other-worldly receptivity, or were we designed by the Nephilim, (those who cane down), as mentioned in Genesis 6:1? Could it be that Shiva was a Nephilim? What I discovered is that when you first make contact with an alien or the other you are immersed in their energetic field. It is my opinion that this alien intelligence field affects the human mind in a very unique way. It takes time for the alien intelligence field to integrate itself into the human mind before one realizes that one's consciousness has changed significantly. This is very similar to the time it took with my making contact with the aboriginal deities. In the beginning, after contact is made, there does not seem to be any noticeable change in our human mind. This alien intelligence field can come about by witnessing a brief sighting a close contact, or even by experiencing a bright orb or even a sudden flash of light.

The deep effects of this alien intelligence field on the human mind will take a long time to become operational within one's thinking. At first, it is undetectable, but after a while, a sense of being different engulfs one's whole body. A sense of having the alien mind is first recognized by a unique feeling of inclusiveness whereby everything we see and hear and sense is somehow all fused as if nothing at all existed. A feeling overcomes one's sense of being where you feel that you are having a unique knowingness that overcomes one's entire mental framework. The difficult part of being able to identify with an alien mind is that there is a constant tendency to attach to some reference point that is familiar such as a particular memory. Physical needs for keeping our human body functioning interrupts the alien mind but only momentarily as this new unified state of mind begins to command our attention. For the most part, this unified mind feels like being in a semi-catatonic state whereby a stasis of sorts seems to fill the identity of who we are which is being part of a new unified state of mind. However, out of this semi-stoic state of existence, a new revelation of life makes itself apparent and the stillness of this unified state becomes alive. Consequently, moments do occur where an idea appears as if it came out of the stillness of space as an undefined momentary coalescence turning into an image or a pattern or a message or even a new form of communication as if voices were floating in your mind. If one remains still these voices seem to be in constant flux as if floating in space. The slightest bit of conscious intention immediately forms word clusters or even sounds as if

7

coming from nowhere. A living dream state becomes real as if a kaleidoscope of knowledge was arranging itself for you to follow. Thinking becomes an entanglement of moods, words, and sounds all creating a symphonic orchestration that seems more like it is coming from outer space, but in fact, it is coming from your own internal mental space.

This is the alien mind operating within us. It is elusive, but it is dynamic, fleeting, and concrete in its effect on how we think. Hearing begins to include the slightest audible difference in frequencies, and seeing creates new forms in the mind's eye blended with changing frequencies giving a feeling of unity without questioning what is being experienced. When speaking from this alien plane of existence words are fully comprehensible when spoken, but how the words are arranged by sound is different from how the content of the arrangement of the words is experienced by the listener. Another alien mind, however, when encountering this form of speech is immediately recognized as another alien mind, and a form of mind melding takes place, which fuses the two minds as a whole universe of thought. Aliens identify with each other when they meet through the way they interact with sound independent of the humans who harbor alien-like other consciousness.

Once you identify with yourself that you have an alien mind the world may appear differently and communication with other humans may feel estranged or even distant. However, once the alien mind fuses with another alien mind an entirely new experience takes place whereby exchanges between two alien minds include all alien minds as a field of intelligence encompassing the universe.

These new human experiences of accepting another alien mind is a new experience that may cause a period of adjustment, because at the beginning of meeting another alien mind we have to learn how to communicate across time and space, and it may at first be difficult to assimilate universal knowledge. The alien mind is universal whereby all communication occurs simultaneously. How ideas are transmitted and organized between human minds becomes the real challenge as individual human minds may be in conflict with accepting the unified field of an alien mind or the mind of the other. However, once acceptance takes place with the human mind as being part of the alien mind, and the relationship between another human who has successfully integrated the alien mind with the human mind a more encompassing relationship begins to unfold.

When I finally sat down behind my tent at the Fowler campground I began to realize that the spot I had chosen looked out onto the forest with Mt. Shasta nearby. I sensed it was an extremely quiet place where all the birds and deer were living in harmony. I was also close to the Lower Falls so I could hear the river flowing down the mountain. One of the most important elements for extraterrestrial contact, I discovered, is to be in a very quiet place with nature, and in this case, I was as close as I could get to nature and Mt. Shasta. There has to be a place where reciprocity can be had with the very high frequency that I have found to be universal among my contact experiences, which I have also had in other remote areas. If you watch the ears of a deer they constantly orient them to the slightest sound.

This same attunement is also achieved with alien contact. Developing the skill to know when contact is being made is what I had discovered at the Fowler campground resulting in a very long contact experience. My first contact came when I was 12 years old. I was living next to the Atlantic Ocean and on a very quiet night, I was contacted by beings who could talk within my mind and showed me the star systems they came from. Now that I am over 80 I have experienced years of encounters with intelligence, not from our planet. All my encounters were very important because who you meet in your life's journey after making contact introduces you to more understanding of the universe. It's because of nearly 70 years of making contact that I can review the social side of the alien encounter by being aware of where you have to go and being aware of who you meet on the way. It was in this still space at Fowler campground that I came to know that aliens were living on this earth.

Chapter Two: Seeking the Vision:

When I first had a mental image of Mt. Shasta is when I was doing Sanskrit translations in Bangkok in April of 2021. I found it quite amazing that one month later I was finally camping at the base of Mt. Shasta at the Fowler campground. I did not know exactly what I would discover next to Mt. Shasta or what I would experience. I thought I would use the time to write another book about my contact experiences, but when I did begin to write I had difficulty developing a narrative. Instead, what I wrote were opinions and points of view which I decided I would write anyway. I was unfamiliar with seeking a vision of something that would come to mind or that I might see. So the writing was a form of exploring how to find a way to develop a narrative. In a way, it was a form of free writing.

This was the beginning of my exploration into ideas that eventually resulted in an awareness of being in the now that eventually led to a meaningful dialogue with a presence that seemed to fill my mind and that eventually became part of my body. I began by writing that we are supra-sensitive humans, which we rarely discover for ourselves because of living with so many distractions our culture has produced. But a unique distraction is the subtle voices that come to mind out of thin air. It could be as simple as what name is to be given to a newborn or as profound as an idea of building a new car or even as extraordinary as hearing how to solve a complex problem. As a child in 1952, I heard voices asking me to take a walk in the early morning hours from beings who had information on where they lived in the starry heaven and said their civilization was in the center of the universe. On December 21, 2012, those same voices also contacted me early in the morning standing on top of a mesa in Chaco Canyon, New Mexico. They asked me if I would tell other humans who they were and how they lived in the universe using sound to travel amongst the stars. Then later, on December 21, 2020, I had a direct conversation at 2:00 am in the desert of Yucca Valley, California with a form of intelligence not of our world using sound to communicate with them.

At that instant, as I was writing about my experiences in the Fowler campground, five beautiful deer surrounded me at my campsite, and my mind raced through decades of former experiences that reminded me of all my contact experiences that I had over a lifetime. One experience in particular, which I had forgotten to mention in my book, Alien Child, was a time in 1967 when the air froze like glass or ice all around me while I was walking and I could see reflections that spanned the universe. The experience took place when I was an editorial assistant for Harcourt Brace and Jovanovich publishers in NYC. I had just left a science building on the campus of Penn State University in State College, PA. As I was walking on the campus walkway everything I saw in front of me was frozen or still as if made of ice or glass. There were walls of glass each reflecting images of each other that cascaded into an unknown realm each reflecting images I did not understand. I felt frozen in time as if living in a giant crystal. Then in an instant, I began walking again as if I had just passed through some unknown dimension.

As my memories were still swimming in my mind a voice called out from the trees, "Catch it now, it's here now, a metal container will stop because of heat." I did not know how to react when hearing that. As evening set in and darkness arrived at the campsite the insight of becoming a voice for others as well as the realization of preparing for contact was what I was writing about. I sensed a gathering of minds was coming together, and I wrote what I heard in my mind, "Give to one's self the total reality to propagate and generate." Instantly a new being emerged before me that illuminated a circle of stones that were placed around my tent. I could feel that I was being affected by the coming of some presence and that a gathering of people was going to take place where some kind of message was going to be delivered. In 1998 I visited a cave in Ipoh, Malaysia which was over one million years old. The stones I collected from the floor of the cave were pure white. I brought the stones with me to the campground and for the first time in 23 years, I took them out of a pouch and placed them all around my tent. The memories of all past contacts became vivid in my mind, and a gathering of people is what made me think.

When I decided to come to Mt. Shasta from Thailand I did so because I had a vision that I wanted to follow. When I arrived in the USA on May 1, 2021, it was shortly thereafter that Jagat Rainbow, a close friend, informed me that there was going to be a conference in Mt. Shasta in late August that I might be interested in. Cameran Frisbee, another close friend, sent the internet link to the conference. I inquired about the conference and shortly thereafter I was invited to be a speaker. I had no intention to go to a conference, but as circumstances unfolded that is what I was going to do. The gathering of people was certainly a reference to that, but possibly a much larger gathering of beings was to assemble at the same time. One evening the Mt. Shasta winds were blowing through the tops of the pine trees creating high-pitched rushing sounds. As I watched the stars straight up through the trees into the heavens with arms outstretched beckoning some arrival of other-worldly entities, I saw a white orb slowly and quietly descending through the pine trees with circular discs illuminating the wind sweep tree tops. It felt like a new recognition of our unification with another species. Slowly the discs descended and an orb appeared announcing the unification of humans and extraterrestrials. Our minds are temples exploring time and space. Orbs of light are condensed

14

consciousness from throughout the universe. It was then that a presence introduced itself to me.

When morning came the sun seeped through the base of the trees rising in the East. I experienced a mind meld of all minds. The alien experience was a life-changing experience, which took time to be fully disclosed. The image of the orb was clear as it descended through the trees. There were no references to compare to this alien experience as it defied any immediate understanding and just presented itself to me in the most unexpected way. Experiences such as these during my lifetime have carried me to where I am today. As a child of 2 years of age, I could not stop thrashing my head from left to right at various rates of speed while the rest of my body lay perfectly still and I could find this to be a restful way to fall asleep. At 4 years of age, I had a complete out-of-body experience and could see myself floating above my bed as I watched myself move around my bedroom. Then at 12 years of age, I was asked to join unknown entities from outer space. I was told at 12 years of age that my new friends were vising our planet because of unusual disturbances in the magnetic field on our planet that became altered. These entities wanted me to discover what caused it and correct it. After a lifetime of contact experiences, I finally realized I had met one of those off-planet entities at the campsite. The orb experience that evening engulfed me and made me realize that all my contact experiences, and especially the orb I saw appear in front of me, left me in a state of shock as I realized all events are integrated across time and spaced. The experiences I felt during my time at the Fowler Campground were unexpected. It made me realize that a vision quest requires a new integration of life's experiences so a new approach to life can be forged. But as the rising sun slowly inched its way up through the trees on the horizon I knew that the making of an image that reconnected and incorporated the fusion of our species with other-worldly beings was appearing in my mind. Immediately I felt contact had been made. In seeking contact it is necessary to keep the acceptance of contact in a state of hopeful attainment rather than an actual contact realization.

Yesterday, I met Rob Potter, the organizer of the August conference, Hierarchy of Light, at his home in Mt. Shasta. Rob was interested in how contact was made, how one recognizes contact, and what you do once contact is made with an extraterrestrial. When contact is made something is revealed. The other life form is revealed at the moment you have the contact experience. We witness our human configuration in the universal now. The universality of knowledge becomes a floating sphere where ideas are extracted from our past and fused with visions of the future. Our sense of time is fused. The edifice of other-worlds spans out into the stars as if a living entity could be seen stretching across an infinite array of starlight. Minds float across the heavens observing

16

the many life forces we lived with as well as time spent on Earth. The life force appears to us when we make contact and are extensions of our mind mixed with other minds in the universe. A collaborative mind tribe comprised of all acquaintances who passed through our lives when we were all on the same plane. But the contact fuses all that and a new reality emerges as our contact experience affords us a different kind of mind that interconnects all our time using memories of all the people we met in our lifetime. Words and names float by with the songs of birds, animals talking, squeaky gates in Paris of a time long gone, and all at once, everything becomes whole. We become an agent of universal consciousness across the heavens. These experiences became a trigger for all my memories and many former experiences became woven into the moment that was being written down on what I was sensing. The technique or way to make contact was revealed as a way to allow our minds to communicate in the universe with other sentient beings. I hoped Rob understood what I was saying.

By this time I became aware that what I was writing each morning was not the narrative I expected but instead it was ideas that were born out of an imaginary state that combined my memories with additional information that seemed to insert itself into what I was writing. It was as if two stories were being written at the same time. One story was recollections of events in the past

17

combined with an additional story that explained things in a new way. It was as if another entity was editing my ideas. I began to write about the sound of words when I heard many voices of past acquaintances who spoke of their ideas. The message I got was to amalgamate all the parts of what the voices were saying. Kim Veltman's voice was heard. Kim was a global linguist who wrote, *Alphabets of Life*. He analyzed all languages that appeared on earth and he was able to demonstrate how our ancestors fashioned a way to communicate with one another by using hand motions and sounds. Then Markus Buehler's voice was heard through protein sounds from his protein synthesizer. The soul of the universe spoke through Stuart Hameroff and Sir Roger Penrose. Bird songs sung by the Cahuilla tribe in the Anza Borrego desert in Southern California could be heard flowing through the Wind Caves. It was a moment when instructions were revealed on how to communicate with other-worldly entities. After 30 minutes under the sun-filled pine trees, a voice exclaimed, "Go back and review what was written". Again a trickle-like-affect consumed me with my mind recalling past voices of ideas that I was previously involved with.

Then a breakthrough took place. My consciousness approached the unknown realm of alien consciousness. The alien spoke and became a storyteller through a portal to my mind. As I kept writing at the campground I found myself projecting into August. August was the month I would be a speaker on how to make contact with extraterrestrials. This event had the potential to convey an idea or a new form of language. It could be xenolinguistics or even the language of the alien intelligence field of consciousness or the language of the soul or even the language of the stars. I was at a threshold or a luminal place whereupon I was entering another realm through the gates of the Symplegades (clashing rocks), as mentioned by Joseph Campbell, or a threshold to another dimension protected by Ganesha. There was a sense of the movement of the planets or even a galactic wind created by the cosmic plasma fields. Who is it that we are attempting to communicate with or have an exchange with that is inherently part of our evolution? A thematic approach I think is how to communicate with other forms of intelligence. We need to be open to anomalous cognitive activity whether it be a sound or an idea or even a vision. How do we go about growing our consciousness to become galactic communicators?

Collectively I believe we are sharing our evolution with the developments of a form of galactic consciousness. The permeating sound of the universe that resonates throughout the universe is the plasma fields that affect the tubulins in our microtubules producing the amazing dance of the 20 amino acids that creates life. Collectively we are sharing the evolutionary developments in galactic consciousness. We are water pods that emit light and sound comprised of all wavelengths. We are cymatic extraterrestrial manifestations communicating throughout the universe. We are little drums pulsating to the rhythm of the universe.

At this point, I realized it's not what we have done, it's what we are doing. You reach a window of myth where everything comes to fruition. The moment you are ready to see the vision it is immediately after the vision you are left with awareness. One has to participate in one's destiny. We are players in a plan beyond our comprehension. Sitting in my chair inside my tent and looking out the tent window I reached my vision quest moment. It felt as if I was in a capsule on another planet listening to what was being told by countless celestial cultures. It was as if I was looking at a microtubule of nature with the wind moving the branches and the plasma fields moving the tubulins as the light moved through the trees. The winds of Mt. Shasta became a journey into self-realization. I found myself in a vision portal. It was a place where new ideas and realizations were happening and the entry of an extraterrestrial fused with my body. I was not taking anything intoxicating or mind-altering substances. I was only full of Mt. Shasta air and water.

Chapter Three: The gathering

Months later I was camping at Lake Siskiyou Campground. In only a few more weeks I would be experiencing a large gathering of people. I did not know whether that meant the people in attendance at the conference or another gathering of people that had something to do with my vision of receiving messages to go to Mt. Shasta. What I did know is that I would be speaking at the 8th annual summer conference of the Hierarchy of Light. I could not help but think of the message I got at the Fowler campground that a large gathering of people would soon be gathering. I could feel the presence of another entity within my body as if I were two people. It was a very pronounced feeling and I could not ignore it. One day, as I was sitting in Lake Siskiyou admiring the mountain I experienced a high-pitched whine that filled my mind as well as a slight audible sound that was flowing in and out of my mind until I heard a voice say, "welcome". Immediately I gave the response, "thank you." It was not a lot of communication but it was an incredulous encounter. I could not help but think it came from Mt. Shasta. The foremost thing on my mind was preparing my talk for the people at the conference. It was going to be the first time that I had ever addressed people who were affiliated with off-planet entities. And even though I had my own direct experiences of entities not from this world I had never made a public presentation to a UFO group. However, it seemed easier to find thoughts that helped me draft a conclusion on why humans were making contact with extraterrestrials.

The experience of having made contact at the Fowler campground helped me to understand more about what a gathering of people meant. What exactly was the reason that so many people were having contact experiences with other-worldly entities? All my life I was living with the realization I had been contacted. But now that I was about to explain how to contact extraterrestrials and the reason we have these contacts was the most important thing I had to do for the people attending the conference. Experiencing a presence within me was another factor I had to accept as a result of my encounter at the Fowler campground. I experienced a similar experience in the Anza Borrego desert in 2016, as well as in Yucca Valley, California in 2020. There always seemed to be some sort of direct extraterrestrial interface as if the knowledge derived from extraterrestrials was already within my body. There was something else that was necessary to be aware of to fully understand this hidden knowledge. Understanding this relationship between humans and extraterrestrials was complex because it felt as if there was a knowingness of the *other* but it was deep within the human body and was hard to access.

To bring a conclusion to my talk, I had to know what the contact experience was all about. What was the reason we humans were being contacted? This question was the most difficult to answer. I knew one thing for sure and that was humans were living on planet earth and another entity perhaps not of this earth was also living on the earth. There had to be some interface between the two but humans could not figure it out. Speculation and hypothetical scenarios were all we could rely on. However, in my case, I did have direct contacts so I knew I was harboring some form of energy that was able to speak to me or present ideas to me as well as generate sounds for me using my electronic synthesizers. It was a Sherlock moment of trying to put all my experiences together to see if a solution would avail itself to me. Was the gathering of people some sort of a test? I wondered many things about the gathering. I wondered if it was a test to see if I could explain the interface between humans and extraterrestrials, or whether I was able to receive information that I would then deliver to the conference attendees. A reciprocal relation was entertained whereby we as humans were able to give to the aliens something they did not have and we in turn received knowledge that enabled us to further our evolution. As humans are biological entities was there something in our makeup the aliens did not have? Were humans acting as surrogates enabling aliens to have offspring? Do aliens need our bio-electric makeup to generate their energy?

The day finally arrived when I was going to present a talk on how contact is made with *other* life forms. It was the most unusual thing I had ever done. I spent a lifetime carrying with me the knowledge I gained from those star beings when I was twelve years old. From a contact in deserts to mesas in New Mexico, I finally settled on the fact that we humans are making it possible for these unknown entities to propagate themselves. Humans are alien baby makers and in turn, we gain access to knowledge that enables us to eventually join them. It was not that it was a definitive answer to why humans are making contact but it had a certain plausibility to it. The content of my presentation followed a timeline of my activities in life. I was not trying to invent a reason for the contact experience but being in the position I found myself in there was a sense of urgency to present the answer. I had never experienced such a difficult task. Searching for an answer came slowly until I realized that the *other* was somehow inextricably a part of my presentation. Whether it was living with the *other* at the same time or becoming part of a field of consciousness in which the *other* functioned was not known. The realization that our awareness of the *other* was somehow interwoven into our very makeup was foremost on my mind. So when it was time to give my presentation on how we make contact I also knew the audience was probably waiting for the answer too. I also could not help but wonder if the *others* were also wondering if I had the right interpretation for how we make contact or if they were dictating what I would say to convey the idea that humans filled a surrogacy role for the *other's* existence.

When my presentation was nearing the end I could feel a strange sensation overtake me. Finally, the reason we make contact took on a very important part of my talk. A new sense of reality took over and I felt that my body was being used as a conduit for another kind of energy. It was a vibration that came over me and not words. I was unsure that my explanation was good enough and instead felt as if I were creating a wave of ideas based on sound and not definitions and explanations.

The second part of my presentation was to create a sound experience using two iPADs. One iPAD had a Tibetan bowl app installed and the other a synthesizer app. The combination of the frequencies from the two instruments produced sounds to soothe the mind and allow a meditative state for the audience. I was still recovering from the odd sensation resulting from trying to explain why we make contact with *other* entities whose origins we do not know. The setup was very simple with only two iPads and a mixer connected to speakers. I felt more at ease with the prospect of making sounds as that was more representative of the distinct feeling I had when delivering my presentation. The transition from speaking to making sounds felt more connected to what it was I wanted to say. This was a very new situation because I was going to try and compose sounds that created a state of mind that would enable a receptivity to the field in which I thought the *other* would communicate. I combined two instruments. One of the ancient bowls used in ceremonies in Tibet and a digital synthesizer that was capable of making many frequencies. The mixer provided other special effects that I could also introduce. This was more than just an opportunity to make sounds. It was an opportunity to see if I could help transport the audience into another realm whereby they could experience their mind exploring the universe.

After 10 minutes I looked up to watch the audience and was startled to see everyone with their heads bowed down towards their laps. Not a single person in the audience was looking at me making the sounds. I did not want to stop so I went back into the rhythms and soundscapes I was creating. It was at this point a new type of synesthesia overtook me. A language appeared in my mind filled with shapes and different spaces. My consciousness became like a stream of light just flowing by as if in some kind of illuminated river of thought. It appeared as a fluid language where everything was connected to something else. I felt removed from my surroundings and just allowed myself to be part of this stream of light and sound. It was a deeper communication than I had ever felt before and voices were coming from everywhere. It was impossible to tell how many voices but it was a chorus of sounds that seemed to be explaining something. Light connected with light and sound with sound and it was all as if a ribbon of spirals just flowing through space. I caught myself looking at the audience again and they were in the same position as before. I slowly faded out of making the sounds and the audience just sat there motionless and completely still. I did not want to say a thing and magically one by one the heads lifted and we all realized we had just been transported to another place but had no idea what happened. I was relieved and satisfied that this type of response took place. The sunlight on Mt. Shasta could be seen through the front door of the hall. I slowly walked outside and was transfixed with what I saw. The towering peak of Mt. Shasta gleamed in front of me and I had to wonder who the audience was.

Chapter IV: The Origins

How did the mind, which was created out of the universe, develop the ability to communicate back into the same space that enabled its creation? The distractions and the combined knowledge that has been accumulated over the millennia have at times produced civilizations that have communicated with the stars but at the same time, so many distractions exist keeping the mind away from communicating back to the stars. One such people who have communicated with the stars for over 50,000 years are the Adyamathanha aborigines from the Flinders Range in South Australia. The aborigines call the space in which they communicate with their deities the Dreamtime. The Dreamtime is a fusion of the natural forces into one celestial whole where every part of the earth and heavens is inextricably connected to every other part of the universe. The Adnyamathanha and their two deities, also referred to as the "lawmen', look over their people from a place in the heavens known as the Magellanic Clouds. The Valnaapa live on the exoplanet Proxima b. within the Megellanic cluster of galaxies. The newly launched James Webb infrared telescope will be observing this planet for life-supporting elements something the aborigines have known for thousands of years. A few years ago I took a trip to Iga Warta, Australia to meet the aborigines and participated in their Dreamtime. I was fortunate to meet the elder Clifford Coulthard of the

Adnyamathanha tribe and through him experiencing the Dreamtime became a reality.

As I said earlier, Dreamtime is a fusion of all the natural forces. The actual dreamtime and the aborigine's Dreamtime are the same. A process of initiation and acceptance has to be established first with an elder before experiencing the Dreamtime because the aborigines can see into your body as if it were just composed of space. I took all my electronic music equipment with me to Australia because it was the other language tool that I was familiar with. Clifford told me I would not have immediate contact with their deities as it takes time for any messages to reach their abode in the heavens. When I began to make my sounds there was a distinct feeling of being enveloped by another domain. There was a strange mysterious space that seemed to be created within the space I found myself in but it was a different space. The space felt like a special world where everything was blended and constantly moving. I recorded my communication to the deities but could not stay a long time. Clifford told me if I were to be contacted I would have to wait several weeks or even a month.

And then it happened. Waking up from a dream is normal but waking up in a dream was a new experience for me. The landscape was the same I had visited when in Australia but I was not in Australia anymore I was in my condo in Bangkok. But the dream was very Daliesque. The grass was radiant green and the oranges on the trees were as big as pineapples. In the distance, there was an enormous spiral staircase that just vanished into the sky. But suddenly things changed and I saw two extremely tall brown stick-like figures descending the staircase. They had to be over 20 feet tall and started to walk toward me. As they looked down upon me the ground around me began to move and the hills changed into clouds and the two beings turned into stars. I was suspended in space. I became a person that had no shape but was just composed of space, but in that space, I still could think. There was no reference to what I was only that I knew I was alive and could see that I was among the stars. Where I was going or where I was from didn't matter as I was connected to everything. Illuminated pathways could be seen connecting the stars and the two deities stretched their arms crisscrossing the heavens, It was a lattice structure of pathways all illuminated between the stars. My head rolled over onto the grass and I just woke up under an orange tree while still in the Dreamtime. Then I woke up again and immediately realized I was just in the Dreamtime. Clifford said I would have contact, and I knew after my dream that I did make contact with his celestial entities who lived on Proxima b.

The universe is a cosmic plenum that pervades everything. Out of this plenum are the origins of everything so it's extremely important to fathom this realization. When the astronaut Edgar Mitchel saw the earth against a backdrop of stars, when he went to the moon, he commented that he felt that the molecules of his body were the prototypes of an ancient generation of stars. In other words, he felt every part of the universe was constituted in his body. Edgar Mitchel went on to establish the Institute for Noetic Sciences in Sausalito, California which is where I met him. The plenum acts as a quantum language that communicates through a network of stars which coalesce into a reflective field creating sentient beings. In my book, *Alien Child,* I described how voices instructed me as to which stars in the universe they came from. That early encounter affected all my future experiences enabling me to present these ideas that are embedded in my mind to this day. Consequently, a part of my reflections is conjoined with the reflections of entities that have influenced my mind and have even become a part of it. I have always remembered that evening in Nahant, Massachusetts when I was told by voices in the sky where they were from in the universe.

In time I built an environment resembling a cylindrical chamber similar in shape to the unidentified aerial phenomenon (UAP), called, Tic Tak. These Tic Tak were recently photographed by navy pilots in 2017. But the film chamber was built in 1968 with a curved screen creating the illusion of 3D images. It was a very productive experiment as I could imagine I was in a spacecraft that felt like I was an entity traveling in the universe. The whole point of building these simulations of mock spacecraft was to explore as many possibilities as I could to understand how it might be possible to become sensitive to a form of contact we are not familiar with. The film chamber was just one of many constructions I built over the years to simulate this experience of traveling in space while trying to understand the *others*. Creating visualizations of many types either with film chambers, sounds, building mock spaceships, or even elaborate diagrams were all done to initiate making contact with extraterrestrials.

Ether Ship console 1973

The most elaborate construction to emulate a spacecraft was a mock spaceship called the Ether Ship. The design idea for the Ether Ship was a result of seeing a cigar-shaped craft hovering over a country road at 2:00 am on a cold wintery

morning in Minnesota in February 1972. I stopped the car and stood outside and

saw small circular windows with shadows of the occupants inside. The craft

was very bright and it slowly moved to the left and disappeared into the cold

night sky. I was quite shocked and when I got back into the car I rushed to the

University of Minnesota. When I arrived I sketched everything I saw. However,

after a week had passed I began to have vivid dreams of what seemed like

blueprints to make a simulated spacecraft. The craft I built was a musical

instrument, but there were attachments to the instrument that incorporated a

brain wave analyzer, color organ, small tesla coil, two argon lasers, and a

portable AKS electronic music synthesizer from electronic music studios

(EMS) in the UK. Based on the colors created in front of me and the sounds

from the synthesizer and Hammond M3 organ I was able to monitor my brain

wave frequencies. A notation system was created for integrating voice and

color. When a different sound was made, with the color that was projected by

the color organ, the frequencies on the brain wave analyzer changed. The lasers

were used for illuminating rotating crystals causing light images to be projected

on the concert hall walls. I toured many universities in the United States with

the Ether Ship before settling in a studio in the Haight Ashbury of San

Francisco. The use of the color organ and the lasers were important aspects in developing a new language for communicating with extraterrestrials.

However, even earlier than the construction of the Ether Ship I received an invitation to participate in an art show at the Howard Wise Gallery on 50 W 57th street in NYC. It was a gallery show titled, *Propositions for Unrealized Projects,* held September 19 – October 10th, 1970. As a result of my contact experience of seeing a white orb appear out of thin air and leaving me with impressions of a more advanced race of beings I was able to design an elaborate magnetic spacecraft called the *Magneto Pod.* The Magneto Pod was a spacecraft composed of magnetic fields that were controlled by a database for any contingency that would serve the occupants. Included in the Magneto Pod were an electronic synthesizer and a color generating machine. The Magneto Pod was designed by connecting two half spheres that acted as landing pods and living quarters. It is interesting to note that all three constructions of the cigar-shaped film chamber, a mock spacecraft, and the Magneto Pod were all influenced by having visual contact with an unidentified aerial object. In some way, an impression was left in my mind so I could build, draw or even compose electronic music as a result of making contact.

In later chapters, I will discuss these psychological effects as a result of having made contact. In the examples, I have just explained each contact

34

experience left a different impression. In many ways, it was as if I was driven to complete tasks due to the impressions the contact experience left with me. In my early childhood, the impression left to me was that *others* were living in the galaxy and universe that have been able to find our planet and influence our evolution in dramatic ways. As a result, I was always looking for the most futuristic activities to become involved with. Today thousands of sightings are taking place all over the world and we learn daily of people having new encounters. Collectively we are being left with impressions from the *others* that will result in new ideas and innovations to help our species evolve to prevent our extinction.

Chapter V: The music of nature

Thousands of beach stones pushed back and forth by the tides created a chorus of undulating white noise outside my childhood bedroom window lulling me to sleep every night. The constant sound of waves and the morning calls of seagulls provided me with an early introduction to the audible rhythms of nature. While watching the deep blue hues of the sea and listening to Beethoven's pastoral symphony in my bedroom a world of orchestral variations accompanied by the undulating white noise of beach stones floating in the air. The symphonic world I created enabled me to participate in the imagery created by the sounds. One night while watching the reflections made by Graves lighthouse projected on my bedroom walls through the Venetian blinds a voice spoke to me and asked me to go outside for a walk. The rest of my family was sound asleep so for some reason I agreed and quietly tip-toed outside my house into the night sky twinkling in the heavens. The voice then said it would like to show me where they were from by telling me where to look in the night sky. The voice talked to me for a long time and I even fell asleep on the rocks next to the ocean. My father found me the next morning and took me back to the house. That was in 1952 and now I am writing this in 2022.

I went to Cambridge, Massachusetts in 2019 to visit Dr. Markus Buehler at MIT. Markus is an extraordinary scientist who spends a lot of time looking at protein molecules with instruments that look as if they may come from some other world. Markus found a way to convert the movement of the protein molecules into sound eventually recording over 100,000 of them which are all cataloged in the protein data bank (PDB) accessible on the internet. The Protein Data Bank is a database for the three-dimensional structural data of large biological molecules, such as proteins and nucleic acids. However, what is extraordinary is Markus took the sounds of the 100,000 proteins and created a protein synthesizer that you could play like any other electronic synthesizer. Markus asked me if I would like to have his synthesizer to be used in my electronic synthesizer compositions. Naturally, I agreed, but what happened after using the protein synthesizer forever changed my entire conception of sound and how it plays such an integral part in who we are as life forms in the universe. Recently published was the most detailed model of a human cell to date obtained by using x-ray, nuclear magnetic resonance (NMR), and cryoelectron microscopy datasets referred to as cellular landscape cross-section through a eukaryotic cell. It was accomplished by Stanford and Harvard researchers, Evan Ingersoll and Gael McGill. Inside the human cell, there is a signal protein that sends out a particular frequency to the 20 amino acids that create all the proteins that make up the human body. So in a sense by playing the protein synthesizer I was hearing the sounds that constitute the very structure of my own body. It may sound strange but when I played the protein synthesizer I could feel the proteins in my body were in resonance with the frequencies from the protein synthesizer. The proteins in my body were actually in communication with the sounds of the proteins made by the protein synthesizer enabling me to experience my life on a new level as now I could, in a sense, hear myself for the first time. The being who was me was creating a resonance frequency with itself as a result of playing the protein sounds that also existed in my body.

For the first time, I realized my sound body and I immediately recalled Edgar Mitchel's comment about his feelings when looking at the earth in space that the molecules of his body were the prototype of ancient star systems. It was at that moment I realized I was a sonic being in communication with other beings in the universe. My body was composed of a river of frequencies all flowing though me and coming from everywhere. If I heard a bird calling then I became that bird. If I had a thought that thought could be coming from anywhere in the universe or any other universe. The minute I made that sound of a protein on the protein synthesizer that part of my body was in communication with every other part of my body. I was riding my sound signature. The finite world and infinite world were in constant communication. If my thoughts were of the *other* then I became the *other*. Becoming multidimensional with multiple personalities simultaneously gave me a more holistic identity. I was not used to experiencing so much input at one time. The protein synthesizer provided me with more capabilities to communicate with the dimensions I found myself capable of participating in. Becoming more than one person was easier to assimilate. Remote projections were normal and with the sounds made from my synthesizers I was able to travel on those sound landscapes very similar to the model of the cellular landscape. There was an opening to expand a sense of individual self to a universal self.

This new realization did not come without a lot of conscious adjustments. If the sound of cricket was combined with a bird song it created a state of consciousness that was so comprehensive only by meditating very frequently could I calm my excitement? Where did the voice come from on Lake Siskiyou and who was the being filtering through the trees at the Fowler campground? I know I am not the only one who has had to deal with these questions of self where another reality overtakes you. A point is reached whereupon I could travel through all past experiences and connect with how each event contributed to the overall realization of the complexity of our cells, which is the complexity we have to relate to. We have all reached this new reality. We live in multiple images, multiple sounds, multiple sufferings, and multiple joys. We have become a new type of human and just now we are learning how to combine our thoughts to connect to our race. The new sounds being made over the planet are an extension of world music into true space music. Now we have to navigate our new world and develop a better way to evolve.

All the UFO and UAP phenomena that we see force us to try and explain what we have seen. We try to explain it to others but in most cases what we try to explain cannot be fully understood. The white lights or white orbs we experience directly or see moving in the sky leave us perplexed for the rest of our lives. Trying to give voice to our experience leaves us with an inadequate attempt for a believable experience. My experience with directly encountering a white orb left me in shock for several hours with mild hallucinations and a lot of physical discomforts. The following explanation has resulted in my own interpretation of how witnessing a white orb made me think very differently.

I relate to the orb as a xenosphere, which I define as a volume of space existing inside the human head. Inside the head, there is a grey-like substance that has electrical fields running through it. This grey matter filters all cosmic radiations as well as responds to sound which enables fields of energy to traverse the entire brain instantly. The xenosphere, therefore, is limitless in scope as it mirrors the space outside the brain which encompasses the total space in the universe. The interaction of the xenosphere with the space around it is the source for how we can create dimensional music and quantum states of consciousness. The xenosphere also can assemble an infinite array of electrical discharges to form a holographic virtual environment composed of a myriad of perceptual images. These images form percepts that respond to sound allowing the percepts to release their configurations so they are absorbed into the xenosphere. When this transition takes place from percepts to occupying the entire xenosphere the percepts fold into a constant motion of energy. Within the xenosphere this motion translates into a sound field containing phonemic language elements. These phonemic language elements instantly form an information network that is in constant motion transporting the phonemic elements waiting for a pulse from the infinite space surrounding the xenosphere. This pulse causes the xenosphere to create concepts and percepts which can change instantly. The concepts are fleeting and exist to be further extended to form complex philosophical approaches to identifying the universe through new cosmological interpretations. This is the source of insights, ideas, and inspiration that can be captured on paper using symbols comprised of writing, sound compositions, visual representations, and other forms of expression contributing to a subjective state within the xenosphere. Creating sound representations of the motion of the phonemic structures is a way to phase with the pulsations from the universe that cause the xenosphere to discharge its electrical activity for constructing percepts and concepts. The xenosphere also has a direct connection to a sound-producing function that can be used to communicate with other xenospheres in the form of languages, pictures, telepathy, and sound. The language component of the xenosphere is a way to provide an exchange of information on any scale existing in the universe. The semiotic function of the xenosphere is in a state of qualia whereby the subjective activity transmits that state of qualia through various forms of expression. The source of the pulsations directly affecting the xenosphere can come from any direction in space stimulated by a myriad of force fields currently understood to be operative in the universe. The xenosphere is responsive to these external pulsations even the internal pulsations that are transmitted by a self-referencing system within the xenosphere.

As humans we not only are affected by pulsations inside the xenosphere but additionally, we can directly interact with these pulsations outside the xenosphere. This interaction allows sound to be converted into a sonic field of conscious activity. This interaction of self-created sounds and the sounds induced by the space outside the xenosphere is a way to explore multiple dimensions existing in space from any time frame. Within the xenosphere are sounds coming from the interconnecting networks existing within the brain's matter. One of those networks currently being explored is the sounds of the folding patterns of proteins created by amino acids forming complex protein structures which enables the xenosphere to maintain its existence. Now it is possible to subjectively interact with the elements which hold the xenosphere together along with the pulsations coming from space. Any dimension is now available to the electronic music composer due to a symbiotic relationship with the formative fields of energy existing in the universe causing these pulsations which are in turn reflected in the xenosphere. The pulsations come from the micro and macro worlds enabling the composer to traverse these worlds using multiple forms of dimensional expressions. The resulting sounds, therefore, represent a form of sonic architecture or dimensional space music. The audible sounds come from the pulsations existing in the universe which directly impinge on the xenosphere. The xenosphere contains a vast array of sonic dimensions allowing a way for sound to follow any path leading from the micro world to the macro world on any scale enabling the composer to traverse those worlds by creating multiple dimensions of sonic expression. These sonic networks within the xenosphere mirror the connections in the brain that allows our state of consciousness to come into existence. Dimensional music is ultimately a form of expression which is responsive to pulsations from the universe as represented within the xenosphere. The white lights in the sky or white orbs are a reflection of our brains living in the universe. These are speculations and intuitive insights that come from thinking of how we have become newly evolved humans. Our thinking encompasses a collective not only with other humans but with the sonic beings traversing the universe who are the *other*.

Chapter VI: The language of the universe

Flowing through the mind of humankind is a constant rhythm of every sound that traverses the universe. Sonic energy fills the universe as it does our body. Understanding how the sonic universe relates to the sonic energy of our body is the basis of a language that is shared with all matter in our daily lives and the universe. The sound of cells and the sound of stars are directly related. Another way to look at the universe is that it is a phonemic and phonomic universe. The phoneme and phonon define the universe as a primordial world that contains the meaning associated with every atom and molecule that has been fabricated to communicate with itself. The slightest variation, however minute, not only by sound but also in the way the sound has a language that speaks from the entire structure of the universe. This is the domain of awareness in which sonic beings communicate their responses to the dynamics of the universe. The awareness of what humans are born into as a domain of conscious activity is barely understood. The sonic complexity in which vibrations are responsible for the reality humans are born into is barely considered. The umbilical cord that connected us to our bodily origins is replaced with a new umbilical cord once our eyes are open. The light that floods into the brain is not only filled with photons but phonons as well. The evolved combination of these two elements of photons and phonons in the universe brings about synaesthesia of experiences that forms the thought world we live in today.

However, the instant another life form interacts with a human a drastic change in the arrangement of those sound and light elements gets modified and assimilated into a newer structure of conscious activity. This physiological change is a real change that is experienced, but the ability to function with those innate changes is when human consciousness becomes interrupted. New perceptual changes occur as a result of new attempts to fabricate reality to relate to those perceptual changes. This then is the current state of global consciousness we are experiencing today. The millions of sightings and personal contacts infiltrating the human race and creating a new renaissance of human conscious activity. An effort is underway to communicate with these off-planet entities and understand how to interpret the communication we are receiving from them. It is safe to say we have reached the level of a new hybridization of the human having one part comprised of earth-bound understanding mixed with a galactic and universal understanding. The fusion of the scientific mind and the so-called aesthetic component of the mind, more commonly known as artistic expression, is revealing a massive display of the result of that fusion.

One fusion contributing to that hybridization that has altered the field of musical composition is the integration of the electronic sound synthesizer. This instrument can easily be used or acquired by anybody. However, the sounds produced by these electronic instruments have been used only as an accompaniment to the classic modes of music. Langauge exists worldwide producing a myriad of sounds that could be produced to foster a global race that can translate the same meaning with the use of different sounds. The ability to make sounds for communication with another race of sentient beings has now evolved into the discipline of xenolinguistics rather than linguistics. Xenolinguistics is being developed to better understand how to communicate with the *others* and linguistics is for human language understanding. How to communicate with a language based on xenolinguistics is aided by electronic synthesizers. The invention of the protein synthesizer was a significant contribution to expanding the concept of xenolinguistics. Taking sounds from deep space captured by radio telescopes and infrared telescopes and then sonifying those frequencies that are outside the realm of human hearing has created additional ways of listening to the universe.

Creative adaptation to a language used by the *other* is an assumption that a new sound could be used as a higher-order language that the *other* would be capable of understanding. New thought synthesis is directly connected to new frequencies. The megalithic civilizations all over the world used sounds created by stone dolmens and wood fashioned into sound-making instruments. Always there has been an attempt to connect to a higher order of existence other than that which exists on earth. One only needs to stand in the center of Chartres cathedral, as I have, to feel what the pipe organ does to our realization of a higher order. There has always been an attempt to create a sonic portal to another world. This is the place in history we now find ourselves in. After millennia of making sounds, we now are creating a new language to evolve with a new kind of celestial knowledge that we can use to redefine who we are as thinking beings. If we are to communicate with the *other* we are now prepared because the assumption has been made that it is possible.

By contributing, ideas for celestial communication come as a result of having made contact and having experienced mental and physiological changes. The thoughts we experience through making contact are directly related to how we create newer symbol systems either by sound or in writing. The *other* uses a holistic approach and any form of communication is based on that universal involvement with energy. Soon billions of humans will be in direct communication with one another on a universal reflective basis knowing that our thoughts are a part of a unique human force field that can radiate into space to phase ourselves into experiencing a new relationship of life in the cosmos.

Before that happens we will see the creation of activities that bring us closer to a more comprehensive field of awareness. Currently, on Bandcamp, the electronic music group Ether Ship has created a way for sounds to create newer pathways in our minds for thoughts to restructure themselves and be able to become sensitive to a new language created from force fields made from the elements in the universe as well as the sounds embedded deep within the cells of our bodies. Once we consciously participate in these realms of the micro and macro worlds we will give birth to a life form that goes beyond the boundaries that we experience today with our level of knowledge.

Chapter VII: The future is now

We live in a field of sound that permeates our entire body. The collapse of time and space has enabled our consciousness to be everywhere simultaneously. Within that universal space is a language of constant change that communicates a direction for our imagination. Our current awareness of being surrounded by another intelligence is offering the race of humans to grapple with newer possibilities to define the universe we are living in. This unification of thought spans all time and is a result of the infiltration of a consciousness that has been developed by a more inclusive consciousness that we see appearing all over the planet in the shape of white lights, triangular shapes, and tubular containers. We not only are living with the *others* we have become to a large extent sharing their intelligence with our own. The process of a symbiotic relationship between the *other* and the human is accelerated due to the inability of the human to support their life support system which is planet earth. The extinction of languages from indigenous people as well as the extinction of other living things have permanently jeopardized receiving the immense variation of knowledge transmitted to earth and converted into usable energy through living things. It has become necessary for the *other* to enter the human body because they have a direct connection to a race of beings who have been able to harness the energy that flows throughout the universe. To replace these lost frequencies emitted from other life forms it has been necessary to provide the understanding of using technological innovation that can capture not only deep space variations of energy but also the minute molecular realm of animate and inanimate matter.

The bonding that is now taking place between the *other* and the human has finally reached a level of recognition by humans leading to innovative approaches on how best to understand how we can communicate with our celestial companions. Human intentionality has been the de facto operating system by which humans have guided themselves. Driven by self-identified needs for organization and control over our perceived destiny for survival has not produced a cohesive planetary overall approach to long-term survival. Human extinction has taken on new importance because it threatens human survival. Only recently has a global system developed, however, the current globalization bringing the world together has still ignored a long-time survival strategy by ignoring the disadvantaged. Unfortunately, it is the realization of not being able to accept the real meaning of an *other* form of life existing on the planet, which is different from humans and has not been fully acknowledged as a collaborative relationship for our evolution and survival. Nor has the intelligence being offered to the human race by the *other* to grapple with newer possibilities been recognized as a real contribution to our survival. That is not to say that the contributions being offered by the *other* are being ignored. Rice University in Houston, Texas has created the *Archives of the Impossible*, which is a repository of the research done by many scholars who have dedicated their lives to the phenomenon of the *other*. Significant archival contributions have been made by Jacques Vallée, Whitley Strieber, Diana Walsh Pasulka, and Sebastiano de Fillipi from Argentina.

However, collecting data is different from realizing that our species has already undergone the biggest evolutionary change that can be recognized by everyone if we are willing to accept this hybridization. This realization allows us to speak from a position of consciousness that is a hybrid consciousness consisting of the *other* combined with the human, To avoid extinction the intentionality of humans has to be guided away from self-serving interests and channeled into an unimaginable potential that is currently being supported by the *other*. The *other* is giving us the understanding of that universal potential to live with a consciousness comprised of intelligently guided fields rather than guided by self-serveing interests that we are currently asked to adapt to by systems of governance. Humans are now in a spawning relationship with the universe. Our ideas and imagination are being instilled with a plethora of ideas and suggestions to aid in giving the human offspring a newer family of consciousness that is space-based and not solely earth based. Many examples exist showing us how space manifestations are being created such as the James Webb Telescope which allows us to explore the deepest realms of space.

Ashley Zelinskie, an artist based in Brooklyn, NY, has created a 3D printed art work showing arms protruding from the golden mirrors of the JWT. Zelinskie comments on her artwork describing how humankind is reaching for the unknown. The JWT allows everyone to share in the wonders of the universe enabling us to expand our place in the universe. Likewise, atomic force microscopes enable us to peer into the molecular structure of the building blocks of life everywhere on the planet. Ashley states, "The abstract idea of studying what you don't know is hard to grasp. This is a disconnect that art can help fill in. Art asks people every day to think about abstract ideas and opens a doorway for creative thinking. I hope to apply this open-mindedness to science and in this way be better equipped to take in the universe in all its vastness and mystery."

This quest by an artist to explore the unknown is also a goal of the *other*. Even though innovations may not be recognized as a contribution from another more advanced life form. It is worth considering as a possibility. For those who have been contacted, accepting that there are meaningful alternatives to the confusion that has caused anxiety with understanding their difference from other humans is not a psychological impediment. This new consciousness I am suggesting is a result of all my personal contact experiences. A new acceptance that our human nature has been affected by the *other* is a first step in exploring new ideas that come into existence while using our thoughts to define who we are. The sound element is one of the most important to recognize. From ancient times to the present the ability to use sound as a transformative element in our conscious development is critical in elevating our place in the universe.

Linda Eneix of the Neolithic foundation in the UK asks why civilizations 11,000 years ago incorporated sound into megalithic sites. Acoustic archaeologists and neuroscientists confirm a significant change in conscious activity results when these megalithic stones are struck. The assumption that a global change in consciousness took place over 11,000 years ago affecting the consciousness of humans all over the planet is something to seriously consider. A frequency generated from some galactic activity changed the direction civilization would take. This awareness combined with the knowledge that we are sonically connected to other life forms allows us to understand our new awareness. Soon our whole relationship with humanity will change and our adaptation to that change is now being seen and felt worldwide in entirely new ways in how we communicate. Our thinking changes and our relationship to the way of the world is also changing. The biggest change will be when humanity realizes that there is another kind of intelligent life form on the earth that humanity recognizes. How that realization transforms into a new identity for humankind is when our potential to harness the innovations that are given to us will be used for this higher form of a human being that can live with a conscious adaptation to *others* in the universe. It is impossible at this point to imagine what that may be like in real time for the human race but fantasy and science fiction have paved the way for imagining many new possibilities. Now civilization has advanced to produce instruments that can make sounds that resonate not only with the sounds of the universe but even with the sounds made by proteins in our bodies.

It is possible to make contact by recognizing the differences in perception that are constantly taking place worldwide. However, the difficulty to harness those changes in thought is not being dealt with very well. It requires a focus and a realization that we can evolve into the same beings that are currently here on our planet. It requires that we can recognize the *others* who need to be communicated with as I am attempting now to do with you. It is the changes taking place in the inner self that has to be recognized.

Chapter VIII: The consequences

What will the consequences be like when we finally accept another sentient life form into the human family? Speaking from my own experience I think it is a difficult thing to do. Collectively as a race on earth we have accumulated a great deal of knowledge and wisdom. We can see what ancient cultures have done over thousands of years and we can witness what the human race is doing in the early part of the 21st century. For the most part, the wisdom we have gained and the actions we see do not match very well. Confidence about a peaceful future we can all live with seems out of reach. Fear and hope about the arrival of the *other* are met with mistrust or salvation. The collective will has not been able to accept that we are evolving to explore the universe. However, many of us have been infused with another form of intelligence, including myself, that gives us the feeling and a knowingness that we are not alone and harbor the very intelligence we seek from the *other*. Many of us are the *other* and that realization is difficult to accept on a personal level and more difficult for humans to accept as a possibility. Because of these psychological and physiological effects on the human body with having made contact, and as a person who has lived with this unknown feeling, I know how difficult it is to understand, I completely understand the frustrations that go along with it.

When the US navy pilot, Ryan Graves, photographed and described what he saw when chasing one of these white orbs it stretches our belief system forcing us to admit we are living with a phenomenon that challenges our place in the universe. Graves described a translucent sphere with a cube inside of it which was verified by others in his squadron. My intention in this book is to focus on the psychological aspects when having an encounter or direct contact. The first thing that is usually done is trying to explain what was experienced to another person. What is discovered is that we find ourselves lacking the vocabulary to give the experience its proper identity leaving the other person you're talking to not being able to believe what you experienced and is not willing to engage in any further discussion. There is a sense of being alone with what was experienced even though the encounter or the contact changed our lives to such an extent that we are left doubting what was seen or experienced and retreat into ourselves forever. We end up carrying with us a permanent neurosis of just feeling out of place. This state can last for years forcing us to carry the realization that things are quite different but have no access to a voice or find an outlet for our sense of change in our makeup. However, the best solution I have found over the years is to stay vigilant and maintain a sense of curiosity in recognizing the fact that you believe what happen was real and that you allow yourself not to suppress the experience. The most prominent psychological effect is disbelief. We have no mechanism to deal with strange-looking humanoid shapes or seeing lights dancing in the sky, dreams of another world, or voices dominating all our thoughts. There is an immediate tendency to find a way to just forget what happened. On the other hand, the physiological effects are much harder to ignore. Abductions cause personal trauma, and body entering is extremely uncomfortable. Nervousness and extreme states of anxiety are all part of the effects people have experienced.

My most traumatic experience was when another entity was trying to enter my body. I fought very hard trying to get rid of whatever it was that seemed to get inside or under my skin. I felt paralyzed and unable to move. I never considered it an abduction but it was a foreign bodily experience. In another incident, I came close to a white orb that left me with extreme hallucinations. I was feverish and could not control my actions. My friends had to hold me down as I wanted to do unusual things such as walking on tabletops in a restaurant or thinking that all the parking meters were alien monitoring devices. My world became very unfamiliar to me. Another state of alien presence is when a momentary state of paralysis came over my entire body and I found myself made of reflections rather than flesh and blood. All of us have had these experiences. In time hints or flashes of clarity pop into the mind and immediately fly away. The most pronounced personal effect is talking to yourself. There occurs an internal dialog and a new kind of intuition that forces you to do something you had not thought of doing such as taking a trip or looking up a person you never met, or getting involved in an activity that was not part of your interest area. It becomes confusing to think and a struggle to deal with the new ideas that fill the mind.

This is the phenomenon of the *other* occupying our mind and body. There is a fusion of the *other* with us and we become a hybrid entity finally realizing we are not the same person we thought we were. Now that there are so many sightings worldwide as a result of social media capture devices a new reinforcement to accept our different nature is slowly becoming a reality. How does one accept a cube in a sphere flying in the earth's atmosphere as seen by Ryan Graves in front of his cockpit window? The tendency is not to accept it at all even though the most sophisticated technology can record its existence. But it is not the external object I am focusing on but the psychological and physiological. These are the conditions that millions of people are dealing with. The feelings of being rejected, shunned, and ignored by others are common personal exchanges after experiencing the first contact. There is a real sense that people can feel the difference in a person who has been contacted and usually the topics of discussion are different. The Questions that are asked are clues that the other person is different but does not understand why. A state of consciousness is finally reached where the realization that there has been a change is accepted. The change I speak of is one of accepting the fact that we have become hybridized.

We are not AI clones we are aliens in a human body. Saving the human species is extremely important as we are bio-space organisms guided by the force fields in the universe and we have the potential to evolve out of the earth cocoon into the space cocoon where all manifestations of a universal existence reside. Not only are we being prepared to evolve but the *other* needs our bio-space organism to thrive as well. Planet earth is the incubator planet providing the connective relationships to communicate within the universe. Not only do we have to recognize our hybridization we also have to utilize our newfound consciousness that is produced by such a relationship. For me, it was a sound relationship for others it may be a remote viewing relationship or a genetic splicing relationship. Every hybrid has a proclivity to help evolve our species so we do not go extinct.

Currently, there are millions of hybrids on the planet. As the ancients 11,000 years ago were affected by a sonic trigger that elevated consciousness, the same trigger will happen to all the hybrids by another sonic trigger or EM wave or some gravitational stimulus. Each of us needs to be prepared to assimilate this change of identity to relate in a more holistic way to the *other*.

The frequency rates washing over the planet are changing our behavior patterns drastically. There is also new insecurity with the relationship to cultural identities. The global change is blending all the various modes of consciousness leaving most unable to find any peace within themselves. Religious doctrines, although valuable to give sustenance to the soul of humankind, are being replaced by the soul of the universe, which is becoming a reality that is extending our earth-bound concepts. A universal soul replaces the human soul in as much as our new existence is part of the larger soul. We are flying from earth to space with a new realization. We become the guides for those evolving into a new world. The virtual world we have created morphs into the universe where a new experience enables us to see differently. So it is essential to recognize our change, accept our hybridization, and capitalize on our new consciousness to prevent the extinction of the human race.

Chapter IX: Change agents

What happens to the way we think when a real encounter with an *other* not from our planet takes place? The reality is that the encounter is not immediately understood and disbelief is more natural than feeling you have made contact. But in truth something does change throughout the entire body and encountering an alien life form requires understanding on how change may take a long time to be fully recognized. The encounter can come from many different directions and sources. It can come about by being associated with another person who has been changed or you may find yourself in a different environment or space that interacts with the change agent that is already within you. A change agent is the subtle energy field emitted from the *other* that interacts with the human body and causes a change in behavior whether psychological or physiological. The change agent can also come from a sighting or the influence brought about by actually having made contact.

Most of the attention surrounding the extraterrestrial phenomenon concerns itself with the objects that are detected in our planets air space and whether they are hostile or friendly. However, very little attention is devoted to the psychological and physiological changes that effect the human body when contact is made. These experiences are highly subjective in nature and trying to live with the experience or communicate a changed state of mind to friends is usually fraught with feelings of inadequacy or incompleteness. One aspect of this change agent that has infiltrated the body can be dealt with if there is some ability to orient toward what is called self or self-awareness. The self is a very malleable phenomenon because the self is a field of energy that is always changing. The extraterrestrial change agent inserts itself into the human self. The problem is that the comprehension of the human self is not fully appreciated. Self-realization and the pursuit of a state of mind that is clear and balanced is a highly sought after place to be. The Hindus spend a lifetime trying to attain Atman which is the spiritual life presence of the universe. Within that clarity of mind the change agent exists operating as if your true self was operating without any interference. But if a question is entertained as to whether there are other life forms in the universe then this is a first step to discovering the change agent. There has to be an intentional introspection as to the likelihood that the *other* lives within us and among us. This is a very difficult place to be because it forces us to admit that we are not alone and are willing to explore the possibility of contact. This is a first step that can be referred to as a mental contact. It's a subjective state of mind where you allow yourself to accept another life form into your life. The next step is to see if it is possible to find a way to determine if you are being contacted. How one goes about to explore this contact depends of course on the individual. The graphic illustration by Walter Steding on the cover of this book depicts how I experienced a walk in entity from another civilization using frequency modifications to create a language that could be exchanged between the *other* and the self. This becomes a private exchange and one that needs to be considered as a reality and not to be denied or thought of as nonsense. Any mode of language exchange can be used by the *other* for this contact experience. In the film, *Interstellar*, there is a dust storm and Cooper's (the lead actor) daughter, Murph, deciphers the dust patterns falling on the floor as Morse code, but later it is determined to be coordinates of a secret NASA headquarters. Likewise in the film, *Arrival*, the markings made by the alien Heptapods were in fact logograms designed by the mathematician Stephan Wolfram and finally used in the film as the alien language to be interpreted by the actor, Louise Banks, in her role as (Amy Adams) the xenolinguist.

These subtle identities made from other intelligent life forms is exactly what we have to do to uncover the change agent that is operating within our bodies. For me it was when I heard the sound from my first electronic synthesizer. After many years of using many different types of synthesizers I finally felt as if I could hear sounds independent of making sounds. Different voices and sound waves would flow through my mind and I was able to replicate those sounds with the synthesizers and travel to different dimensions.

The take away from what I am trying to say is the ability to be sensitive to very subtle changes with your own conscious activity. All kinds of energy fields are affecting animate and inanimate matter which is being modified by this energy. We have the ability to relate to any subtle energy fields existing in our bodies as a direct reflection of the energy fields in the universe.

How our attention is diverted to focus on something we normally would not pay attention to is one way the *other* effects the sense perceptions of a human. Another way to describe this attempt to communicate with the *other* is recognizing a cognitive anomaly or something different than from the way one would normally think. It is as if a hunch was amplified to a state of prescience, remote viewing or even clairvoyance. How reality is constructed is a key aspect to sensing if there is a different way of seeing the world. Fortunately we now live in an era where we are integrated into knowledge banks through the technology called the internet and artificial general intelligence (AGI). But this external technology may be implanted in our bodies by the *other* so thought and knowledge are simultaneous for information access all over the planet as well as data feeds coming from all space probes being sent into the universe. These newer technologies are definitely a byproduct of the *other* who already has access to all this knowledge. But with the recognition of the *other* within us we can more clearly see how burgeoning technology is part of evolutionary technology needed for humans to become a space faring species. Once we accept the reality that the *other* is a part of us is when the effectiveness of the change agent will change our lives. Consequently, we will be able to share simultaneously all thoughts originating on our planet and have access to the intelligence of the *other* existing with the energy fields in space. How we utilize the change agent is a personal decision based on personal interests. The overall goal of the change agent is to help humanity survive so consciousness can be universal for our species.

As an electronic music composer, I created a platform for other electronic musicians to collaborate with one another. The platform is called, *The Electric Well*, and it is part of the global digital art event called, *The Wrong Biennale*. located in the pavilion, *inAbsentia*, created by Lino Mocerino and Francesca Guiliani from Foggia, Italy. In this way anybody could listen to one composers work or many works at one time and experience a wide variety of frequencies without having to own or use an electronic synthesizer. This was done to take advantage of the frequencies originating and produced by artists from different countries around the world whether it would be Zigo Rayopineal from Argentina or Markus Buehler from MIT in Cambridge, Massachusetts.

Accessing as many frequencies as possible counters the extinction of languages and the sound making qualities of other species. The change agent coming from the *other* can be accessed by recognizing newer ideas that come to our minds. Total abduction and body entering intrusions are the most extreme ways the *other* enters the human body and these experiences have been well documented over the last 50 years. However, the mental repercussions resulting from subtle change agents is just as effective. There are many different types of psychological profiles that the change agent produces and adapting to them requires a sensitivity on how we have changed or how we attempt to describe or relate to our different moods and feelings. A few of these states of mind resulting from making contact with the other that creates a change agent are worth pointing out.

Attention diversion: Modern media technology interrupts the continuity from one subject to another subject. The focus used on receiving information from one source is immediately changed to another subject from another source. There is no relationship of the content that is constantly being delivered through all media outlets. Multiplied by billions of people experiencing no relational information creates a state of mind of attention diversion. This diversion causes the *other* to insert new ideas to attain universal intelligence which is constantly being interrupted by fractured media dissemination of information. When ideas are experienced in the mind with no similarity to any former idea attention diversion is created. This is how a random state of consciousness is created leaving one with a nervous condition requiring sedation to calm the mind. The conscious mind of the *other* is a holistic mind that traverses the universe where all time is simultaneous. Any thought created is a complete thought and follows a growth path that encompasses more energy fields than the human is capable of assimilating. Solutions to this change agent has caused the development of AI as a substitute for human access of thoughts that are constantly changing. However, it will be necessary for humans to entertain the fact that this is a form of intelligence not of this earth and it is a harbinger to the eventual transformation of the human species into a newer type of consciousness.

Memory accumulation: Another effect of making contact is the change agent effect on how to access our memories. A noticeable condition as a result of humans having made contact with the *other* is recalling past memories on a continual basis. The fragmentation of receiving information primarily from the media is causing a sense of anxiety. Memory has been activated as those are fixed and are easier to rely on than the reality we are experiencing in the present. But memories can be made of sound that harkens back to where an event was accompanied by a favorite song. The memory becomes a substitute for the present causing the present to be overlooked or not even considered important. Current reality is replaced with a better memory so that more familiar events from the past give a sense of stability and wellbeing. However, when a past memory is connected to a present reality or even a future projection the entire collection of thoughts are simultaneously mixed together making for an incomprehensible sense of how to interpret reality. Escaping from this fractured mental world causes extreme behavior of renunciation, drug overdoses, and virtual world immersion take over. This phenomenon of memory accumulation is a way to construct a preferred world and an exercise of making time shifts to past events mixed with present events. The solution is not to retreat into a fabricated world but experience the world as a stream of thought. How the energy of the universe is utilized will be a key factor in how all events from any time frame are easily dealt with. Memory accumulation is a result of the *other* educating humans about the time dimension we are capable of experiencing and dimensions that will become very familiar to us as we learn how to navigate different time constructs in the universe.

Tense less reality: The opposite of memory accumulation is tense less reality whereupon there is a sense of no past, present, or future. It is the equivalent of zero gravity of time where there is no form of reference to anything only a constant sense of now. This condition creates a sense of being lost because there is no place to go in the mind except to experience the present as a multitude of sound, color, and shapes. The immediate is the only thing that has any meaning and as long as the environment provides a stable place for the human to exist then the force fields that are emanating from everywhere are the only stimuli that is required to feel one has an existence. Mystics were very comfortable with this state of mind as it was as close to what was considered to be an enlightened state. But in the modern world, the contact experience creates the change agent of a perpetual state of now. Over stimulation is the only way to fill the vacuum of the endless now and as a result, a planetary hedonistic lifestyle replaces any semblance of idea creation or memory manipulation. The *other* has been able to instill a state of emptiness as if floating in space with nothing to relate to. This is the place where the consciousness of the universe exists and the state of mind created by this change agent is another quality needed to attain a universal consciousness. The modern film company Netflix produces endless episodes and seasons, and the video games constantly move from one scene to the next as if nothing ever changes. Nothing is fixed and everything is fluid. This feeling of being lost can be seen on the streets of many cities in the world where people just do not know what to do and cannot find stability in, their lives and are categorized as homeless. But in fact, these people are floating in a universal space content not to have to pick and choose between one thing and another. Remedies for such side effects of a tense less reality are to educate people about where we are in the universe and introduce a more

70

comprehensive overview of how the technology introduced by the *other* has given humans a deeper understanding of the universe. This is how to solve this social situation by becoming a space-based education society so meaning in a new universe can be entertained.

Paranormal sensitivities: A remote viewer by the name of, Ingo Swan now deceased, and my friend, was able to see into the future and paint images of unbelievable cosmic landscapes. Another change agent as a result of the *other* making contact with humans is the ability to experience things in different time zones. But it is not only Ingo Swan who saw into different dimensions. Many people find themselves believing that they come from different civilizations located in distant galaxies or star systems. The contact by the *other* with humans has produced thousands of UFO groups and many sacred sites around the world such as Mt. Shasta in California or Mt. Uritorco in Capilla del Monte, Argentina. Authors Brad and Sherry Steiger published *Real Visitors: Voices from beyond and parallel dimensions*, which is a complete account of the new paranormal abilities many people are experiencing worldwide. Children are demonstrating prodigy-like talents in many academic disciplines. The ability to find ways to communicate with animals and insects is not uncommon. The change agent in this case is a heightened sense of awareness. Hearing voices is one of the most common as well as being able to predict

71

future events. This change agent gives to humans extraordinary visionary experiences which can contribute to being prepared for more encounters with an alien race. The literature is extensive on how humanity will react to seeing these visitors from other worlds making themselves visible and known among humanity. Many believe this is why all these anomalies of human behavior are indicators of a shift in planetary consciousness.

These are just a few examples of new behavior patterns existing as a result of the *other* making contact with humans. In writing about these changes I am aware that I am contributing to explaining the differences that exist among humans as a result of the contact experience people all over the world are having. My contact experiences have varied from hearing voices, seeing orbs of white lights, cigar-shaped crafts, body walk-ins, and hearing sounds that transport my sense of place in the universe. All these change agents and many more are creating a different type of human on the planet. We see differently, think differently, feel differently, and it is difficult to meet other humans who have had a direct change agent experience.

Chapter X: How the *other* thinks

In 1970 I read the book, *Lateral Thinking*, by Edward de Bono. Now 52 years later I am trying to describe how the *other* thinks. It seems like a preposterous task to believe that there could be any way to describe the thought process of another life form, especially one that is not from our planet. The ability to even think this is possible rests on the fact that from an early age I had a life-changing experience that forever caused me to wonder about a civilization not from this earth. It has been a lifelong search of finding a way to understand another race of people and how my life unfolded and the ideas I gained along the way. Lateral thinking changed how I experienced the world using the asymmetric thinking that De Bono described. De Bono's ideas shifted my worldview dramatically and helped take my thoughts as possibilities to where there was a way to communicate with another race of people. The next thinker that changed my way of seeing the world was James Gleick and his 1987 book, *Chaos:Making a new science.* Both authors were very interested in patterns and how patterns can reveal more understanding of how ideas and nature work together. The 52 years that have passed since 1970 have seen so many changes in how we see the world that it is as if we live in an entirely different world. In many respects, we do live in a different world in large part because humankind now has accepted the fact that there is another unknown intelligence that has been seen and recorded around planet earth. This book describes the personal encounters I have experienced and how it has changed my thinking and the effects it has had on my person. The change agents mentioned in chapter IX indicated how to identify the significance of or a different behavioral nature to our sense of self. How the *other* thinks is a recognition and acceptance that the way we think of the world has been caused by the way the *other* has infiltrated our thought processes so we can envision the future and entertain a new form of reference to who we are as humans. To look upon oneself as a hybrid that combines the sentience of another lifeform with our own has a parasidic quality to it. This acceptance of sharing oneself with an alien intruder may sound unacceptable, ridiculous, and impossible. But if one were to take self-thought into an asymmetric realm and entertain the possibility of two lifeforms fused to form a different set of agreements of who we are then a plausible outcome results. The process of thinking with the *other* is a process that takes time to assimilate. Pattern thinking is the ability to integrate a high rate of conscious activity into a change agent of a new comprehension of one's place in the universe. In 1869, Charles Joseph Minard was the first thinker to introduce data visualization as a way to represent complex data in one visual. His ability to visualize the invasion of Russia by Napoleon in 1812 set the stage for modern infographics. Pattern recognition was taken to a new level and now in the 21st-century data visualization is the preferred way to interpret thousands of bits of information into one infographic. The development of the human to process millions of bits of information is a direct result of the *other* fusing with the human. Quaint names were initially introduced to describe this new ability such as becoming a knowledge worker or a data miner. The ability of the human to cognitively connect to any part of the brain instantaneously where information is stored is a technique fostered by the *other*. Elon Musk has developed Neuralink a small device that is inserted into the brain to help run electronic devices just by thinking about them. A term I coined to describe instant data interpretation to help understand the change agent more completely is defining the access of multiple thought systems as a "shift register". This is the ability to access all thoughts on a particular discipline and then be able to shift those thoughts of one discipline to another fully registered thought system. Being able to immediately switch to all thoughts constituting another discipline is a process I refer to as shift register. Switching back and forth between whole thought systems and then being able to access those thoughts at any time is the ability to shift to any previous thoughts that have been registered in the mind. Other terminologies used to describe thought functions are 3D topological thought vectors, deep learning, or even spatial cognitive rotations. The *other* enables humans to easily access multiple cognitive reference points on any subject simultaneously allowing us to become experiencers much like the intelligence of the *other*.

Humans, for the most part, define three states of matter as solids, liquids, and gases. However, there are five states of matter with the other two being plasma and the Bose-Einstein Condensate (BEC). We could say the latter two were brought into human consciousness by the *other*. The *other* has a complete understanding of how to exist in a plasma state as well as existing in the BEC state. Two interpretations of the physics of the universe where one is defined as the standard model of physics and quantum field theory are defined as the other. Jacques Vallée proposes the sixth state of physics which he calls the physics of information. Vallée sees the world as a universe of information with human consciousness becoming aware of the information from microsecond to microsecond. With these three states of matter and three types of physics, we have the knowledge to navigate within the universe much more easily. In an interview with retired Harvard University astrophysicist Rudy Schild by 8 News Now Las Vegas, in 2020, Schild suggested that our intelligence is within the universe experienced by the *other* and the *other* is here on earth experiencing our intelligence (https://youtu.be/P9SBxy-mAoY). Schilds also referred to an overall cosmic intelligence that is being exchanged by both humans and the *other*. I mention these comments by Dr. Schild as a way of

76

showing that he intuited the relationship between the *other* and human without having a direct contact experience which I am assuming Schilds has not had. The pervasiveness of the global contact experience is increasing the intuitive level not only for the experiencer who is affected by the change agent but is also being sensed within the greater population. As I mentioned the *other* has been able to relate newer technologies to humans that have elevated our understanding of the universe. The quantum world has permeated all aspects of science as a driving force underlying all matter and consciousness.

Outside the world of science, a new area of quantum aesthetics was introduced by the Spanish writer, Gregorio Morales. A group was formed in 1999 in Paris, France called the Quantum Aesthetics Group. Morales and his team recognized that there were elements within the structure of quantum mechanics which were affecting the types of artistic expression that were being produced around the world. Most revealing was how the artists were taking quantum elements and incorporating them into newer forms of artistic expression. In the book, *The World of Quantum Culture*, edited by Manuel Caro and John Murphy, Morales outlined the manifesto of the quantum aesthetics group with a chapter titled, *Overcoming the limit syndrome.* It was in this manifesto that Morales indicated the quantum signs to look for that were part of the elements in the artist's work. Esentially, the elements of the universe were mixed with familiar elements on earth but instead of exact representations many of the elements were mixed in such a way using mythology, altered representations of familiar objects, and a surreal interpretation of existence. This art was providing viewers to see different arrangements of information without having to develop higher thinking skills. Any contact by the *others* that would be experienced the first time and cause a change agent to affect their consciousness would lessen the effects of any disorientation that may be forthcoming for the experiencer.

There are many artists who display quantum realities in their work. Larisa "Morysetta" Murariu, from Romania, is a surreal digital artist. Morysetta represents the unknown and unexplored and uses space to depict the subconscious. In her piece, *Mind Traveller*, there is a clear depiction of outer space with new realities detected in some fantasy world with a young girl looking at what seems to be an impossible reality. This mixing of two worlds is indicative of that quantum element of non-locality where you can be in two worlds or even two universes at the same time. Another aspect of the way the *other* thinks is the emotional component of being human. In the abduction literature, there are a lot of personal accounts where invasive techniques are experienced. As I mentioned there are various ways a contact experience can come about. The walk-in experience can be much less disturbing than bodily exploration techniques. But my account of a surrogate experience challenged the way I thought of my emotions but not so much for me to understand but for the *other* to understand. I was performing in the early morning hour on December 21, 2020, at 2:00 am with my electronic synthesizers in the desert in Yucca Valley, California. It was the Winter solstice and it was very chilly but the idea was to make sounds during this significant celestial event. The pedestals holding my iPADs loosened in the cold temperature causing the tablet computers to fall out of their mounts. I was able to catch two of the tablets before they hit the ground and one fell into my lap. The one that fell in my lap I was still able to play and it was also nearing the end of the composition I planned for. As the ending drew near with the electronic sounds I noticed that a higher-pitched tone was coming out of my speakers. I was using my microphone to match the high- pitched whine and soon it felt like my voice and the synthesizer sound were in some sort of communication. The fact of using the microphone and my voice was not unusual but what was unusual was I felt as though I was holding a baby and not a tablet computer. When the composition ended I found myself shivering uncontrollably. I knew I had been contacted because I had experienced physiological effects before and it was a very familiar feeling. Directly after the music ended my relationship with the stars changed. I could see moving lights going past my eyes and I felt a deeper bond with Cameran Frisbee, a friend who came with me. I wasn't giving birth to a baby but later I knew that the bond I had with Cameran was to nurture a relationship that dealt with how parents react to having a baby. I became aware that the *other* wanted to explore my emotional reactions as I tried to bond with Cameran as if we were going to be parents. The experience was a very difficult one because the reciprocal feelings were nonexistent leaving me with feelings of being rejected. As the bond with Cameran became more intense within my emotional makeup I finally ended up having extreme convulsions that seemed uncontrollable. It was as if I was trying to expel something from my body. Eventually, I realized it was an invasive attempt by the *other* to explore my emotions through what I perceived to be my reactions to parenthood. Over time the extreme reactions I had processing the invasiveness of the *other* diminished. As I have said earlier I believe humans are surrogates to aid in the development of the *other* so they gain human attributes. The experience brought me closer to understanding human love and made me understand how much of a difference there is between human emotions and the needs of the *other* to learn about human love.

How the *other* thinks will in time become more familiar with humans. My nature of having a change agent affect my life and bring me closer to understanding my hybridization I think will be a phenomenon that will have to be dealt with by all of us as planet earth assimilates the intelligence and wisdom of the *other* so we can evolve into a spacefaring civilization.

Chapter XI: Personal disclosure

It is probably impossible to estimate how many people worldwide have had some kind of experience dealing with an unidentified phenomenon or a close encounter experience. And of those who have had a contact experience of some kind, the majority never take the time to communicate their experience to friends or acquaintances. I for one can testify that it has taken me a lifetime before I could develop a language to describe my feelings after my first encounter as a child. That first experience has sat with me all my life and I wondered what could have made me walk outside of my home in the early morning and talk to voices who said they were from the stars. That first experience has now been revealed to me through a felt sense of awareness resulting from all my experiences in life coming together allowing me to understand how that childhood experience changed my life forever. One revelation that has come to my attention is that during most of my life I have researched what others have discovered after they had a contact experience. Whether it was driving to Arizona to see, Travis Walton, after his abduction or traveling to NYC to visit the remote viewer, Ingo Swan, it was always to seek out what had happened to others. However, when the realization occurred that the contact experience I had as a child changed my whole person is when it dawned on me that the change I speak of was more conversion than a change.

Accepting the realization that my person was not the person I identified with but another person who was not my person but a person from another world is what created a paradigm eureka moment for me. In many ways, it was a fantasy experience trying to extract me from a reality I could not believe in the acceptance of that new reality as a given. As I write my story I am aware that I am revealing a personal state of mind and only when my book is published and goes public will my story be known. Maybe then I will hear that others have gone through a similar conversion of being changed into what I call the *other*. Maybe I will meet a community of people who can share their stories of becoming an agent of another life form in our universe. I have to admit it is a very delicate balance orienting one's sense of self to one of disclosing to yourself that you're not who you think you are. After the eureka moment I was left with the awareness of the possibility of harboring another kind of selfhood that had existed within me for so many years. The idea of entertaining a dual personage was mostly just a simple exercise in my attempts to understand the lasting feeling that something was different inside of me at the core of who I was. Such a complete change in my identity did not come easily. I knew I had played electronic music in remote locations in the world, or tried to express my thoughts with my first book, *Alien Child*. But when the question of wondering about what happened in my childhood and then adding up all the previous contact experiences is when a new sense of identity just snapped into my consciousness. It was a stunning awareness because I saw the world through a different set of eyes. I did not feel all that much different except there was a new feeling of immediacy or a more active relationship with time. How you own yourself to be a new person is what is most difficult. There seemed to be a need to create more ideas and find a way to build on thoughts to create something new. There is a built-in sense of participation suggesting I am engaged in a mission or a goal that must be achieved. It is a very new experience in writing these thoughts down for the very first time as I am disclosing or trying to disclose an alternate being that has fused with my mind and body. Living with this reality is not new as I have recorded many experiences that would most likely lead to this conclusion. Once in 2012, on Winter solstice, I went to Chaco Canyon, New Mexico, and climbed up a mesa to view the stars. It was a very cold early morning while staring at the heavens when a voice called out and said, "It's nice to have you back Willard." Immediately my mind raced back to my childhood when a similar voice asked me to take a walk. Then the voice said, "We would like you to describe who we are and how to communicate with us." The voice went to great length explaining who they were and that I needed to explain their existence to other people. I took up the request and over the next eight years published four papers on how sound communicates with extraterrestrials in the Journal of Technoetic Arts, Roy Ascott editor: Vol. 12, No. 1, 2014/Vol. 14, No. 3, 2016/Vol. 16, No. 1, 2018/Vol. 18, No. 1, 2020.

After the publication of Vol.18, I felt I had honored the request to document my experiences of encounters with extraterrestrials. Yet even with documenting my encounters the full realization of accepting how I related to myself as a hybrid human harboring another sentient being from another world was not an acceptable reality. The waiting aspect of feeling as if I were an agent from another civilization or another form of consciousness in the universe is what struck me as the most plausible possibility. Multiple possibilities were dancing in my mind on how to accept this new entity into my life. But once I realized the reality completely it was as if I had awakened from a dream, left another dimension, and dealt with how to live where my former self brought me. The here and now were the same but it was not the same me occupying the here and now. If this sounds incredulous then by all standards of normality it is. However, with an increased presence of ever more sightings and contacts around the world and given my own experiences that brought me to create new sonic worlds as described in the literature and recorded in real physical time I knew that I had to find a way to fuse these two opposed realities of a real self and a self not of my origins.

Consequently, I became a hybrid self of two entities fused into one. This fusion of the *other* with the human is a way to advance the evolution of both species. In her book, *The Dual Soul Connection: The alien agenda for human advancement*, Suzy Hansen describes a dual soul agenda where advanced technology developed by the *other* can be used by humans. Hansen explains the close interconnectedness with this off-planet civilization where all of mankind is unfolding together. How the off-planet civilization connects with humans is by guiding us to meet other people who have a high level of technological understanding. When exposing the human through direct contact and by seeing advanced technology being used encourages more ideas for humans to use to advance our evolution and prepare humankind for accepting the arrival of global contact. It is interesting that my terminology of a, change agent, and Hansen's use of a, change within, are two ways of describing how the *other* interacts with humans.

What I have revealed has taken a lifetime to come to grips with. But with the acceleration of the energy around the planet and the necessity to save the planet these contact experiences as well as the fusion of the *other* with humans are going to increase until there is a global acceptance of a new life form that is blending with humans to provide a way to successfully advance to the stars. What I have described is being sensitive to the subtle energies that are now infiltrating the planet. The way each person is responsive to these changes will vary. The impossible possibility to be united with another entity from another place in the universe certainly goes beyond anything we have experienced in the past. The awareness may be immediate or take a long time but for sure there is another presence on the earth that is trying to advance our species. How we adapt to the presence or how we react when we experience our first contact will be a totally new experience and the various approaches I have personally experienced I hope can be of some help is accepting their presence.

Chapter XII: Xenophobia

The word xenophobia means to dislike people from other countries or even anything strange and foreign. It can also extend to being fearful of non-human entities not from planet earth. In his book, *Xenophobia*, Peter Cawdron depicts a strange-looking jellyfish or a white light flying across a desert landscape on his book cover. Is humanity fearful of the arrival of extraterrestrials on planet earth? And would meeting an alien visitor be met with fear? There are already many films with the plot of hunting down synthetic humans such as *Bladerunner 2049,* or the synths being chased in the British TV series, *Humans.* And to extend this xenophobic attitude further what would society do if it realized that some humans were not human at all, but were non-humans in the likeness of humans. In otherwords, is humankind prepared for the intervention of non-human entities and allow them to be accepted into society even if they didn't look human. Would it be possible to admit to other humans that you were not human, and in so doing you would not have to worry about any repercussions that may bring harm to you? As I have pointed out change agents caused by contact with non-humans have already alterd people's behavior, and as Susy Hansen says in her book, *The Soul Connection*, change takes place within the whole body and psyche including the soul. Might there be a whole community of hybrid humans on earth or a completely different kind of human waiting to be activated by some central cosmic intelligence that will then go about changing all humans? What I am suggesting is that there are multiple scenarios on how our earth-bound species are going to react to a non-human species as well as how earth-bound species would deal with their sense of change as a result of making contact. There is a twofold concern about this dichotomy of human and non-human that is currently creating many different groups and communities who accept the possibility that non-humans or extraterrestrials are going to be visiting our planet en-masse very soon. Most recently three research groups have been formed to dea with these issues. One is the *Archives of the Impossible,* at Rice University in Houston, Texas, (www.impossiblearchives.rice.edu), second is the *International Coalition for Extraterrestrial Research (ICER).* ICER believes all countries now need to prepare for confirmation that the earth is being engaged by a non-human intelligence and proposes awareness programs be established to deal with the profound issue of contact and its global implications (htpps://icer.network). A third organization is *Allies of Humanity,* steered by Marshall Vian Summers (www.alliesofhumanity.org).

But these are only a few organizations. Protocols have already been established to communicate with extraterrestrials from an organization called, *Messaging to Extraterrestrial Intelligence,* (METI).

Within these four organizations, any scenario that could be conceived by humans has most likely been considered and research facilities are now made available to explore these conceptual possibilities. However, the realization of how society would accept non-humans appearing on a mass scale is not understood nor is a personal relationship to an off-planet non-human understood. Thousands of humans have been abducted and these abductees claim the entities are peaceful and wish to help humans survive but others claim domination and control are the agenda these entities have in mind. Even with these two agendas imposed on the abductors, it leaves a concern of uncertainty as to what is going to happen when these off-planet entities do make a mass appearance.

The personal transformation I have attempted to bring forward in this book as a result of my personal contact experiences is to explore our personal experiences that have made us become experiencers. I can already surmise the trust factor that will also be a concern. If we as experiencers reveal how we have changed then we may be subjected to unfair scrutiny, as I may be, when my ideas are published. Many people on our planet are involved and admit that there are those of us who sense we have changed so all we can do is to recognize that change in a positive way knowing it is best to ensure that we can help humanity to survive. To be aware of our behavior as a person even though we may be non-humans is another consideration. It is conceivable that we could become biological AI entities and, therefore, we would not be human but would we still be a person? How many humans are there that look like a person but are not human? If we met a person that did not look like a human would we feel comfortable relating to them? I think we would feel uncomfortable. And if I have agreed to become a non-human entity can I still look at myself as a person? The paradigm shift in personal identity will come about as a result of dealing with our xenophobic feelings toward an off-planet entity. We may become afraid of ourselves and not trust who we have become due to our change from having a contact experience. We are dealing with interspecies development and are becoming 21st century Southeast Asian mythical figures the Kainnari and Kainnara a half bird and half human. I mention these mythological figures because they come from the Himalayas and watch over the well-being of humans as do perhaps these off planet entities. We have either become non-human or hybrid humans with both human and non-human aspects to our nature. But in considering all the information that has been collected about how humans have interacted with off-planet entities it is fair to say some type of change has affected humans. What I have tried to do is convey my thoughts on dealing with the change agent that has affected me since a child as well as direct contact experiences during my lifetime.

So, the first thing that has to be done is to become very sensitive to what we are. To be able to sense any change in any aspect of how we think or feel. Review your thoughts and see where they take you. Become related to yourself in a new way rather than just ignoring who you are. The realization of having been changed may not come quickly, but over time the change agent from a contact experience will take place and a sense of deep curiosity about who you are will follow.

Chapter XIII: Accepting two as one

Becoming a non-human person is not easy. One of the biggest complications is adapting to all the emotional triggers that may not be the same as those experienced when in a natural human state. A change agent resulting from contact with an extraterrestrial can overcome the entire body. However, the autonomic nervous system can still transmit our emotional intelligence. All AI developments struggle to emulate feelings and human response mechanisms in circuit-driven AI because the biological transmission of electrical impulses is more sensitive. The off-planet intelligence needs our human bodies to transmit ideas, but their familiarity with how autonomic fluctuations change human temperament is less understood. Even though we become non-human we can still respond to subtle galactic energy fields. The off-planet intelligence has mastered those energy fields, but the changes in a human body driven by autonomic fluctuations from galactic energy fields are not a part of non-human entities. Humans still maintain that emotional aspect of their human nature even though the non-human entity has fused itself within the human person. Adapting to this biological non-human identity comes with a lot of frustration and temperamental changes. Mood swings and changes in behavior patterns are common in the human community. Once there is a fusion of the non-human energy field into the human body it causes neurological short circuits when the human brain sends messages that humans normally respond to. To feel differently as a result of a contact experience has been documented widely by those who have interviewed contactees who expressed they felt physiological changes. Kevin Day, a radar operator for the USS Princeton, was repeatedly ridiculed for trying to express what he saw and felt after seeing images of unidentified aerial phenomena (UAP) on his radar screen eventually led him to leave the Navy. Unfortunately, there are not that many people who are familiar with identifying these contact changes and as a result, contactees feel uncomfortable discussing it with others, the energy field that distinguishes a human from a non-human is how each entity responds to the universal intelligence flowing in the universe. Our cellular structure in recent years has become more understood. We now know for instance that cells produce audible frequencies as do the protein structures and even smaller elements within our brain called tubulins that change frequency as a result of EM fields that impinge on the body from interstellar space. The conscious mind has expanded in its ability to explore our universe as never before and by becoming aware of these developments we activate the higher consciousness that the non-humans were created from. Activating our consciousness with quantum fields has become a new state of awareness for understanding our immediate reality and the universe. But what do we share with the non-human and what makes us different? How do we recognize and welcome this fusion with an off-planet entity?

When we recognize that we see differently, hear differently, and think differently is when we can begin to ponder if we have changed. This quantum reality that is part of the non-human makeup filters through our body and we barely realize we are operating with a consciousness that is much different than the one we are used to. The ability to accomplish multiple tasks using different memory frames from the past, present, and future is how universal consciousness works. Seeing becomes infinite and hearing becomes acute. The visible worlds translate into solutions for different levels of engagement. Our ability to see and hear things from different parts of the world using the internet adds to an understanding of ourselves. There are many speculations about why these UAPs are in the air space covering our planet. The information we have is very limited in helping our civilization to understand this phenomenon. But being a contactee from, an early age and having experienced multiple contacts is the reason I have decided to relate my reactions as a possible guide for others. The knowledge that there have been many civilizations on this planet besides our own is hotly debated, however, scholars like Graham Handcock and Matt Lacroix in collaboration with other scholars are convinced they did exist. The civilization that was uncovered by archaeological excavations at the Göbekli

Tepe site in Turkey indicates not only was there another civilization but also some event that caused it to disappear. But not only are these questions of past civilizations important for understanding our civilization but the questions are being raised as to whether off-planet intelligence was a direct cause for former civilizations to come into existence. The difficult answer to that question is the same as questions being asked today about the existence of off-planet sightings so prevalent worldwide. Connecting dots and speculating on the similarities between a civilization's past and one existing in the future, such as ours, results in some compelling theories.

The most compelling theory for why we are having direct contact is because of the imminent extinction of life on our planet. It has been suggested that these non-humans are trying to give us the intelligence to cope with how they are activating our higher intelligence to prevent our extinction, which as a race we would be capable of using that intelligence for that purpose. The quantum field I mentioned earlier is experientially a common attribute of the off-planet entities and when fused with human attributes creates a quantum consciousness which inspired Gregorio Morales to form the Quantum Aesthetic group in Paris, France in 1999. However, these quantum artistic creations have to be recognize to learn from the visual and audible framework the artist uses to convey a new form of quantum consciousness. Dr. Merritt Moore, a quantum physicist, and ballerina have been invited to Harvard Universities ArtLab where she is exploring dance movements with a single-arm robot. Moore's understanding of atomic laser physics and large quantum states of light joined with telecommunications, allows her to explore an area of human movement and the movement of light on nanowire structures that has led her to learn about topological quantum information processing. This is a complex concept indeed. However, this is a perfect example of a higher form of intelligence never before explored. To say this is the influence of off-planet interference with global consciousness is not unrealistic given the fact we do not as yet have a working model of how off-planet entities function or even how humans will evolve with non-human interference. As conscious beings who desire to survive it is tantamount that connecting unrelated activities outside the specificities of any particular discipline is the best way to advance our intelligence to solve unforeseeable speculations about how humans will survive. Moore states, "The next generation is going to need creativity more than ever."

So, in summation what I am revealing is that with a direct contact experience we are candidates to experience a change agent that ultimately leads to our becoming a non-human yet still maintaining our personhood. With our off-planet assistance, we will find ways to express ourselves differently so we can contribute to the greater whole of humanity to prevent an extinction event that may be on the immediate horizon but is known by the non-human. Slowly our consciousness will work in harmony with the non-human and we in turn will eventually reach our potential and be able to bring our intelligence further into the universe.

Chapter XIV: Extending reality

Avi Loeb, an astrophysicist from Harvard University has just released his book, *Extraterrestrial: The first sign of intelligent life beyond earth.* Anyone with an internet connection will see that Dr. Loeb has been on countless TV shows, YouTube specials, and hundreds of papers being published. After the University of Hawaii's Haleakala Observatory, using Pan-STARRS1, (wide field astronomical imaging) spotted an object originating from outside the solar system on October 19, 2017, the world was stunned. Controversy as to what the object was gained worldwide attention. Ave Loeb, however, took the controversy one step further and claimed the object was most likely designed by *other* intelligent life in the universe and was a spaceship. The object was named, *Oumuamua,* which means scout in Hawaiian. The excitement stemmed from the fact that it was the first interstellar visitor to enter our solar system or at least the first one detected. A report just released in April 2022 by Avi Loeb and his research partner, Amir Siraj, states that an interstellar object entered the earth's atmosphere in 2014 and fell in the ocean next to Paupau, New Guinea. This has been confirmed by the US Space Command's commander, John E. Shaw, making it the third interstellar object entering our solar system. But it is the theories that Dr, Loeb has proposed about, *Oumuamua,* that has caused a total upheaval in the scientific community, and for those interested in Dr.

Loeb's theories you will find that they are relevant to everything I have been discussing thus far in this book.

As far as Avi Loeb is concerned, *Oumuamua* is artificial and designed by intelligent life outside our solar system. That in itself is a monumental admittance to the phrase: we are not alone. But the world by now knows we are not alone so why is it that Avi Loeb has received so much attention. This one man standing on the earth with the aid of modern astronomical instruments exclaims a spacecraft entering our solar system was designed by intelligent life. This is a change agent for the population of the entire planet. Loeb's contact came through a telescope and analyzed it not to be a space rock or any other thing that most astronomers said it was. Loeb turned the academy upside down and asks us to believe it is an intelligently guided spacecraft. And like myself driving on a back road to the University of Minnesota in 1972 and stopped my car and saw a cigar-shaped white craft with portholes and shadows moving past them leaving me with the thought I saw a spacecraft. A change agent has taken place for both me and Avi Loeb. And as Loeb has received criticism for his ideas they are the same that I encountered by my trying to tell my contact encounter. But as much as Loeb is a member of the astronomical academy at Harvard University his opinions have mattered among accomplished scientists. Loeb provides his reasoning and by the process of elimination deduced that what is left is the possibility that what was seen had all the elements that make it a spacecraft. Loeb does not argue with others or ridicule others but points out his reasoning on how he derived his answer. He admits that our level of intelligence is not capable for the world to entertain the reality of another civilization in the universe.

Not only do we see UFOs and UAPs in our planetary air space we now have a respected scientist telling us that another civilization has entered our solar system. These two realizations bring more credibility to confirming the existence of the *other* from an advanced civilization. But because of his position, Loeb's ideas are respected and our need to understand has the support of at least one member of the academic scientific community. The confidence to extend our reality in the face of diversity from others, who have a limited perspective of the greater picture, is what Avi Loeb is showing to the world no matter how many people may disagree with him. *Oumuamua*, and all the lights everyone is seeing in the night sky cause us to pause and begin to ask questions as did Avi Loeb in trying to offer alternative approaches on how we interpret what we see.

The most disconcerting aspect of recognizing the plausibility of an off-planet entity and civilization is whether they are kind or hostile. In my opinion, this question can only be answered by interpreting the change agent that I am

101

talking about that comes about from one's interaction and the direction your activities take you. I have never encountered a malevolent interaction with the *other*. However, the US Department of Defense has created a new task force under the name, *Unidentified Aerial Phenomenon Task Force (UAPTF)*. The mission is to detect, catalog, and analyze UAPs that may pose a threat to national security. In contrast to UAPTF the *Archives of the Impossible*, a newly inaugurated division at Rice University, collects well-documented historical events and common human experiences that are not supposed to happen but do thus contribute to a plausible, imaginable, and thinkable phenomenon that is close to if not real. The mission of the military and the scholarly researchers have some commonality as they both are curious about a phenomenon that is not well understood. One says they are concerned that security is their top priority the other is wanting more understanding of the phenomenon. If we leave hostel intentions to the UAPTF and the paranormal and unusual phenomenon to the Archives of the Impossible we can devote our time to trying to understand the psychological and physiological effects humans have experienced when they make contact. In the above chapters, I have tried to address certain behavioral anomalies as well as speculative possibilities born out of having a contact experience that affects the human body which I have referred to as a change agent. Jacques Vallée is one of the archivists who donated his research to the Archives of the Impossible. His approach to the unknown and paranormal is to explore the physics of information which is the content-filled energy field in the universe that transmits information. I took the liberty in this book to state that this is the field of intelligence of the *other*. The scale we are dealing with in trying to comprehend this field of intelligence is unlike anything we have dared contemplate. Nobody thought, *Oumuamua,* was a spacecraft and I doubt suggesting we are becoming a non-human is equally radical.

However, the point is we have to address an entirely new relationship to a phenomenon that is pervasive worldwide. We can look through telescopes and sift through digital files but sensing our mind and body at this time in history is extremely important. So many people worldwide are now experiencing some form of contact. Whether it is pilots, astronauts or a farm worker in Peru sightings have caused excitement, a real sense of curiosity, and even trepidation. There is now enough evidence and personal experiences, as I have tried to convey, that suggests we are being contacted all over the planet. I like to think it is because there is a need to raise our intelligence so we can participate in our way to prevent extinction. We possibly are being readied to where all humans will form a collective brain that can communicate amongst ourselves simultaneously, but also find our race being integrated into a higher form of an intelligent civilization. We must keep an open mind and be sensitive to others.

Chapter XV: *Other*

I suppose I could end this book by doing something very bold. I think I will let the *other* speak as if an off-planet entity was talking (*other*). Channeling is the first thing that comes to mind, but this would not be channeling rather, it would be the *other* speaking. As unreal as this may seem I am going to give the last word to the *other* who*about*as made me a non-human person.

"Hello, in 1952 there was a lot of documentation of our visit to your planet. The most popular event of our arrival was when we were seen passing over the capital building in Washington DC in July 1952. We also appeared all over New England and even passed over Nahant, Massachusetts, and visited a young boy and tried to educate him about who we were. We spent many hours with the boy (Willard) and gave him many ideas and insights that he would carry with him throughout his life so he could explore many ideas that we were introducing to the planet. Now, after only a few short years in our time, we have infiltrated many of the institutions in your world and as a result, many attempts have been made to help your species understand who we are. In Willard's case, we have allowed him to be introduced to many of the new technologies we introduced to see how he would respond to our understanding of the universe. We noticed that Willard had made a great effort to find a way to communicate back to us, but we have not tried to be too direct but contacted him enough times that he finally saw that we were a presence on the planet and would soon let everyone see us.

All the technology and ideas we have inserted into the minds of your race have been done to accelerate the conscious ability to become aware that another civilization has evolved to traverse the galaxy and beyond. Willard has, through his efforts, broken through our design intentions for helping humans on the planet and is making an effort to explain the changes we have introduced into human civilization. Willard has finally been able to become part of our conscious intelligence field and is working hard to understand how to master his new insights so that others can understand who we are. As a universal race, we are attempting to introduce as many ideas as possible to act as a catalyst for all humans whether it is a global database such as Google or multiple satellite launches done by Elon Musk so every individual has access to the knowledge we have introduced to your civilization. We enabled Willard, to become part of the International Association of Educators for World Peace (IAEWP), an NGO, where he is now on the board of directors as senior vice president for public relations where he communicates all over the world to other peace advocates (https://iaewp-org.blogspot.com/p/office.html). This is a technique we use for many of the contacts who are taking on roles that assist in spreading the diversity of knowledge that will elevate the intelligence of the entire planet. Willard has communicated with many of the people we are in contact with and those people in turn are in touch with many others. The acceptance of our presence is what is the most difficult to understand. Willard has referred to us in his book as the *other*, as a way to bring attention to another intelligent life form that is not from this planet. Most recently we were able to communicate with Willard through sound by communicating with an Argentinian who visited us on Mt. Uritorco in Argentina. Willard in turn was able to send that message around the world by entering it into another global organization called The Wrong Biennale. Willard's collaboration with sound artists around the world with his, *Electric Well*, enables us to share our knowledge through frequency modulation. Zigo Rayopineal was our contact in Argentina.

Our direct involvement with humans has not always been met with a favorable reaction. We also let Willard explain this to you in his book. The reason for all our incursions into your body space is to better understand your physiology. We need to know the tolerance level and comprehension level in introducing the technology that will prevent an extinction level of the human race as the current rate of arms production, elimination of species, lack of food production and the altering of the weather patterns are not going to allow the human race to reach its full potential. Our next operation on the planet is fusing all minds so the human race can integrate a multitude of ideas to stabilize the planet and continue the rate of intelligence to enter a new form of participation in the universe. Our species uses the fields of energies and frequencies to form an intelligence that can manifest any reality by consciously directing force fields. Your species is very close to this ability. Already you can construct a reality in your brain and by focusing on that image you can bring that image into your dimension. Our species has already reached the level that the dimension you function in has been elevated to a more inclusive dimension where we can see the quantum world as an idea. One of your species, Olaf Stapeldon, saw the potential of this control of the cosmic energy fields and was able to visit multiple civilizations that attempted to reach attunement with universal energy. In his book, *Star Maker*, he was able to map the time scale to achieve a cosmical mind. It was a model indicating the potential of conscious growth in the universe which we are currently making our presence known on your planet. Your species has all the ingredients to reach the early stages of this cosmical mind. It is being exhibited by new ideas that are close to this next dimensional level with the concept of the physics of information, propounded by Dr. Jacques Vallée. Information exchange is inherent in all things and there is a knowingness at every level of dimensional interaction. We visited Willard several times since his early age and we were able to give him instructions to follow so he would receive the knowledge that was necessary to help others become aware of another dimension of consciousness. We helped Willard to produce frequencies that would open pathways for the imagination to flourish in new conceptual spaces. Our civilization is still evolving and like all civilizations, we wish to survive as well. There are enormous energy fields that are always expanding in the universe and give our civilization the impetus to go forward and at the same time add to our civilization when we see the growth of consciousness as we do with your species. With the development of your new James Webb telescope, all humans now can peer into the vastness of space of universal consciousness. It is a vast network of interconnecting force fields that produce new elements all the time. The images being broadcast over your planet from the James Webb telescope accompanied by sound are helping your species advance into the cosmical world of universal intelligence. We helped Willard build his light and sound information capsule that was able to transmit brain waves over laser light by assembling electronic devices through a brain wave analyzer connected to a color projector. We have given Willard many avenues to communicate with others on social media using sound to accelerate information exchange even in space. For space communications, we helped Willard join the International Space Apps Challenge in 2013, sponsored by NASA, whereby, he would send out a series of sounds incorporating the Fibonacci number series at the Jamesburg Earth Station in Carmel, Califonia. This was an international mass collaboration focused on space exploration, which was a unified international effort encouraging diversity in experiences of perspectives. Willard used stellar acoustics to communicate with an off-planet civilization that we provided him so he could be in touch with us over a long period (https://2013.spaceappschallenge.org/project/extraterrestrial-communication-using-synthesizer-and-stellar-acoustics).

What we hope to achieve very soon is to transmit sounds over a network of satellites using sounds that we will send to act as change agents on earth so we can distribute as comprehensive a message as possible to all the internet links that we will have deployed. It will be a noninterference activity as a global satellite collaborative music event that will be established and perhaps even arrange to have Dr. Merritt Moore do her ballet in space. In this way, we extend the ability of humans to extend themselves into space to create events because we have the availability, resources, and technology to make it happen. Every effort is being made by us to elevate the awareness and develop more potential for an advanced race of humans to be prepared for that eventual interspecies unification between humans and non-humans.

We are aware that accepting this new reality will be met with a lot of resistance, but the truth is without accelerating the advancements in intelligence the ability to save the planet will be lost. Reading this pronouncement must be very difficult because it is unlikely anyone is going to believe an off-planet intelligence could have written a book that Willard initiated on his own. So I admit I have taken the liberty to save Willard the embarrassment of trying to explain how this has happened so by me speaking directly I think is the best way to introduce ourselves. Willard already has given much advice on how to integrate our two species, and that in itself was a challenge for him as it has been for him all his life. I think because so many humans have seen us appear in so many places and that people are being contacted that this realization I am sharing will be acknowledged very soon. So when you see those bright white spheres flying over rooftops and trees be aware that they are us with our intelligence radiating out from those glowing spheres. We have been photographed extensively and we even hover over wheat fields and leave a message on the land all over the world. When you do see us we emit a kind of universal knowledge that penetrates your body and some of you will feel more energy than others. Willard has made a good attempt in trying to convey what happens to you when you receive our energy field.

Just as Dr. Avi Loeb from Harvard University has expressed, you have to be ready to see us as a possible intelligent being who is trying to help solve many of the problems that are being encountered on your planet. We are inserting new ideas as quickly as we can so that very soon a coalescence will take place so a newer kind of cooperative race will evolve. That is not to say everything you have done thus far is useless, it is just its effectiveness that has to be seen for what it is and you will know how to change it. My advice is universal for any developing civilization anywhere in the universe. It is just that you will have to adjust to differences in how best to relate and accept that other forms of life have taken place in the universe that has the intelligence to travel in the space outside your planet and we are currently helping you to achieve that goal."

Index

A

B

Oumuamua, 99, 100, 103,

P

Paranormal sensitivities, 71,

Pasulka, Diana Walsh, 52,

Penn State University, 13,

Penrose, Roger, 18,

Personal transformation, 90,

Phoneme, 45,

Phonemic language, 41,

Phonon, 45,

Plasma fields, 19,

Protein Synthesizer, 39, 46,

Potter, Rob, 16, 17,

Prapandvidya, Chirapat, 4,

Proxima b, 4, 28, 29,

Protein Data Bank, 37,

Q

Quantum aesthetics group, 77, 96,

Quantum field theory, 76,

Quantum world, 108,

R

Rainbow, Jagat, 14,

Rayopineal, Zigo, 66, 107,

Real visitors: Voices from beyond and parallel dimensions, 71,

Ribbon of spirals, 27,

Printed in Great Britain
by Amazon